MW01078599

Extra SAT® Math Practice

Volume 1

ISBN: 978-0-578-47174-7

i

Introduction

Hi, thanks for buying this book! As you hopefully already know, this is meant to be a bare-bones supplement for extra practice, not a primary source prep book—see *PWN the SAT: Math Guide* for that —so I'll keep this intro very short.

The questions that follow have all been part of my Daily PWN question of the day service. (You should sign up for that, by the way—it's free! Go here: http://bit.ly/DailyPWN) The topics covered here aren't exhaustive, nor are they proportionally representative of the question types that appear on the SAT. They are, anecdotally, the kinds of questions I've seen students struggle with most.

When people answer these questions on my site, the site tracks the number of correct and incorrect responses. That's the data I used to arrange the questions in this book by difficulty. The later a question appears in this book, the smaller a percentage of respondents got it right. The difficulty levels in this book are _not_ meant to correspond to any ranking in any other official or unofficial book; they're just a nice way to break up this particular group of questions. Here's what they mean:

Level 1	75% or more responses correct
Level 2	67-75% responses correct
Level 3	60-67% responses correct
Level 4	50-60% responses correct
Level 5	50% or less responses correct

This ranking is imperfect for a long list of reasons, including but not limited to:

- People who sign up for the Daily PWN are not exactly a random sample of test takers.

- Users can answer questions as many times as they want. This is not common practice, but it's also not controlled for.

- Some questions have been edited for print (*e.g.*, figures redrawn, wording revised for clarity) so they're not *exactly* what people responded to online.

- Multiple choice questions are far more likely than "grid-ins" to be guessed correctly, but I couldn't think of a good way to account for that in my ranking, so I just didn't.

Still, seeing all these questions laid out in order of difficulty, it does feel mostly right.

After the 125 questions, you'll find solutions in numerical order. The solutions include question categorizations aligned with the chapters in my main prep book, *PWN the SAT: Math Guide.* There's also a quick reference page with all the answers in one place at the very end of the book.

Let's see...anything else you need to know? I don't think so! Onward to the questions!

Heather's math teacher gives her the equation of a line in the xy-plane, and then asks her to perform the following steps:

1. Draw the given line.

2. Draw its reflection about the x-axis.

3. Draw a line that is perpendicular to the reflected line (drawn in step 2) and that intersects the reflected line at its y-intercept.

If the original line Heather is given is $y = 4x - 5$, what is the equation of the line she draws in step 3?

A) $y = -4x + 5$

B) $y = -4x - 5$

C) $y = -\dfrac{1}{4}x + \dfrac{1}{5}$

D) $y = \dfrac{1}{4}x + 5$

What is the value of x that satisfies the equation $\dfrac{1}{x} + \dfrac{4}{2x} = \dfrac{27}{3x^2}$?

A) –3

B) –2

C) 2

D) 3

$$y = 3x + a$$
$$y = -2x + b$$

In the system of equations above, a and b are constants. If $b = a + 15$, what value of x satisfies the system of equations?

A) -2

B) 1

C) 2

(D) 3

$$f(x) = x^3$$

$$g(x) = \sqrt{x}$$

Functions f and g, above, are defined for all $x \geq 0$. If a and b are greater than zero, and $a = b^6$, then what does $f(g(a))$ equal, in terms of b ?

A) b^{18}

B) b^9

C) $\sqrt{b^9}$

D) b^3

Group	Adults	Children	Total Admission Fees
Group A	3x	5y	$70.50
Group B	2x	6y	$67.00
Group C	1x	2y	

The Museum of Science charges different admission fees for adults and children. The incomplete table above shows total admission fees collected from three groups as they entered the museum and the composition of those groups. Which of the following equals the total admission fees that the museum would charge Group C ?

A) $23.50

B) $25.25

C) $26.00

D) $27.50

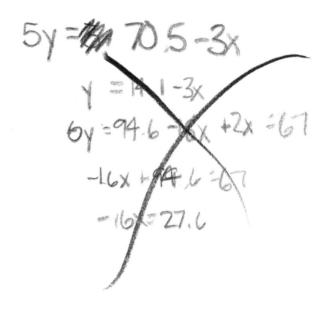

$$y = -(x-5)^2 + k$$

In the parabola equation above, k is a constant. When the parabola is graphed in the xy-plane, its vertex is at $(5, 16)$. If the parabola crosses the x-axis at $x = a$ and $x = b$, what is the value of $a + b$?

A) 5

B) 8

C) 10

D) 16

In triangle ABC, the measure of angle B is $90°$. If $\tan A = \dfrac{4}{3}$, what is the value of $\dfrac{\sin C}{\cos C}$?

A) $\dfrac{4}{3}$

B) $\dfrac{3}{4}$

C) $\dfrac{3}{5}$

D) $\dfrac{4}{5}$

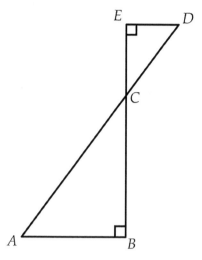

In the figure above, $ED = 3$, $AB = 6$, and $EB = 12$. What is the value of $\sin D$?

$$x + 4y = n$$
$$5x - y = 3$$

In the system of equations above, n is a constant. In terms of n, what is the x-value of the solution to the system?

A) $\dfrac{n + 3}{6}$

B) $\dfrac{5n + 7}{4}$

C) $\dfrac{4n + 3}{9}$

D) $\dfrac{n + 12}{21}$

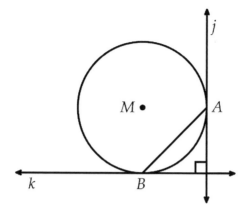

In the figure above, lines j and k are tangent to the circle with center M at points A and B, respectively. If the length of chord AB is $5\sqrt{2}$, which of the following is equal to the circumference of the circle?

A) 5π

B) 10π

C) $5\pi\sqrt{2}$

D) 25π

$$\left(x^{2y}\right)\left(x^{3y}\right)=\left(x^{y}\right)^{a}$$

The equation above is true for $x > y > 1$. What is the value of a?

$$\frac{18x^2 + 15x - 12}{3x + 2} = 6x + 1 + \frac{a}{3x + 2}$$

In the equation above, a is a constant. If the equation is true for all values of $x \neq -\frac{2}{3}$, what is the value of a ?

A) –30

B) –14

C) –12

D) –10

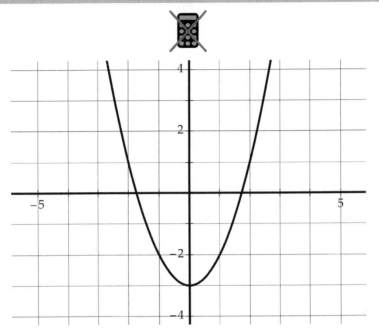

The figure above shows the graph of a parabola in the xy-plane. Which of the following could be the equation of the parabola?

A) $y = (x + \sqrt{3})(x - \sqrt{3})$

B) $y = (x + 3)(x - 3)$

C) $y = (x - \sqrt{3})^2$

D) $y = (x - 3)^2$

Which of the following expressions is equivalent to $\dfrac{x^4 - y^4}{x^2 + y^2}$ for all nonzero values of x and y ?

A) $x^2 - y^2$

B) $\left(\dfrac{x^2 - y^2}{x + y}\right)^2$

C) $(x - y)^2$

D) $(x + y)^2$

The density, p, of an object can be calculated using the formula

$p = \dfrac{m}{V}$, where m is the mass of the object and V is its volume. The

volume of a sphere can be calculated using the formula $V = \dfrac{4}{3}\pi r^3$,

where r is the radius of the sphere. Which of the following

equations could be used to find the radius of a spherical object

given its mass and density?

A) $\quad r = \sqrt[3]{\dfrac{3m}{4p\pi}}$

B) $\quad r = \sqrt[3]{\dfrac{4m}{3p\pi}}$

C) $\quad r = \sqrt[3]{\dfrac{3m\pi}{4p}}$

D) $\quad r = \sqrt[3]{\dfrac{4m\pi}{3p\pi}}$

Seth has some stock market investments that fluctuate in value. The value of one of his investments was $15,300 at the end of the day on Monday and $16,830 at the end of the day on Tuesday. The value of the investment decreased by the same percent on Wednesday that it increased on Tuesday. How much less was the investment worth at the end of the day Wednesday than it was at the end of the day on Monday?

A) $0

B) $153

C) $1,530

D) $1,683

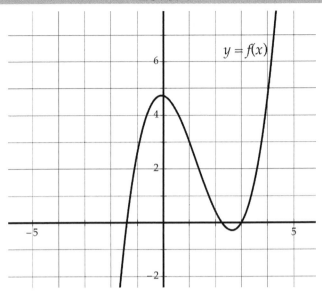

The figure above shows the graph of the function f. If the function g is defined such that $g(x) = 2f(x) - 1$, what is the value of $g(1)$?

A) 3

B) 4

C) 5

D) 6

$$y = a(x - 6)^2 + 5$$

In the equation above, a is a constant. When the equation is graphed in the xy-plane, it passes through the point $(8, 8)$. What is the value of a?

$$\frac{x-8}{x+2} = \frac{x-5}{x-1}$$

In the equation above, $x \neq -2$ and $x \neq 1$. What is the value of x that satisfies the equation?

$$10x^2 + ax - 36$$

The expression above is the product of $2x + b$ and $cx + 4$. If a, b, and c are unique integers, what is the value of a ?

A) -41

B) -37

C) 45

D) 53

$$(3x + a)(4x + a) = 12x^2 + 28x + b$$

The equation above is true for all values of x, and a and b are constants. What is the value of b ?

A) 2

B) 4

C) 8

D) 16

Public Transportation Ridership Statistics

Year	2006	2007	2008	2009	2010
Millions of Passengers	1,461	1,472	1,481	1,453	1,374
Millions of Passenger Kilometers	5,440	5,469	5,501	5,320	5,100

The table above shows ridership data over the course of five years for BKV Zrt., a public transportation provider in Budapest, Hungary. "Passenger kilometers" is a measure of the total distance traveled by all passengers throughout the year. Which of the following statements is supported by the data?

A) The average number of passengers per year was greater than the median number of passengers per year during the period from 2006 to 2010.

B) From 2009 to 2010, the number of passengers declined by a greater percentage than did the number of passenger kilometers.

C) The range of passenger kilometers per year over the period from 2006 to 2010 was about 61 million.

D) The average number of passenger kilometers over the period from 2006 to 2010 was closest to the passenger kilometers in 2006.

Data source: BKV Zrt. Annual Report 2010
(https://static.bkv.hu/ftp/ftp/annual_report/annualreport2010.pdf)

If $i = \sqrt{-1}$, which of the following is equivalent to $\dfrac{14 - 5i}{3 - 2i}$?

A) $52 + 13i$

B) $4 + i$

C) $11 - 7i$

D) $9 - i$

A restaurant owner has determined that in her business selling hamburgers and french fries, she sells two thirds as many orders of french fries in a day as she does hamburgers. She charges $8 per hamburger and $5 per order of fries. According to this model, how many hamburgers would the restaurant owner have sold on a day when she collected $1,734 in revenue selling hamburgers and french fries?

A) 153

B) 144

C) 129

D) 102

If $\left(\sqrt{x}+9\right)\left(\sqrt{x}-9\right)=19$, what is the value of x ?

$$f(x) = 2x^2 - 4x + 8$$

The function f is defined above. What is $f(x+2)$?

A) $f(x+2) = 2x^2 - 4x + 10$

B) $f(x+2) = 2x^2 + 4x + 8$

C) $f(x+2) = 4x^2 - 2x + 10$

D) $f(x+2) = 2x^2 - 2x + 4$

$$0 = (x-3)^2 - 6(x-3) + 9$$

What value of x satisfies the equation above?

Population Growth in Carterville

Year	2014	2015	2016
Population Growth	3.2%	2.8%	2.6%

The city of Carterville measures its population every year as of April 1st of that year. The table above shows the year-to-year percent growth of the population of Carterville from 2014 to 2016. If the population of Carterville was 1,059,382 on April 1, 2013, which of the following could have been the population on April 1, 2016?

A) 1,153,120

B) 1,145,489

C) 1,123,894

D) 1,086,296

Which of the following is equivalent to $\dfrac{26-13i}{8+i}$? (Note: $i = \sqrt{-1}$)

A) $3 + 2i$

B) $2 + 3i$

C) $2 - 3i$

D) $3 - 2i$

For constants a and b, $a^2 + b^2 = 19$ and $ab = 5$. What is the value of $(a-b)^2$?

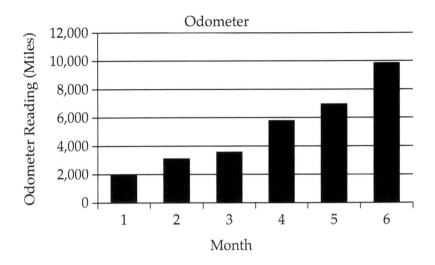

Six months ago, Gerald bought a new car. On the last day of each of the last six months, Gerald has written down the odometer reading (which shows the total number of miles the car has driven). That data is summarized in the graph above. During which of the last six months did Gerald drive the least number of miles?

A)   Month 1

B)   Month 2

C)   Month 3

D)   Month 4

In the xy-plane, the vertex of a certain parabola is at the point $(-4, -8)$. The parabola contains the points $(4, 0)$ and $(a, 0)$. What is the value of a ?

A) −12

B) −8

C) 0

D) 8

If $c^a c^b = c^{12}$ and $\dfrac{c^a}{c^b} = c^3$ for nonzero constants a, b, and c, which of the following is equivalent to $c^{\left(a^2 - b^2\right)}$?

A) c^{36}

B) c^{15}

C) c^9

D) c^4

In the xy-plane, the parabola with equation $y = -x^2 + 4$ has its vertex at point C and intersects the x-axis at two points, A and B. What is the area of triangle ABC ?

A) 4

B) 8

C) 12

D) 16

$$\frac{2^{a-b}}{2^{b-a}} = 4^c$$

In the equation above, a, b, and c are positive integers and $a > b$. Which of the following is equivalent to b ?

A) $-2c$

B) $a - c$

C) $a - \dfrac{c}{2}$

D) $c + a^2$

$$\frac{1}{5}x - \frac{1}{15}y = 4$$

$$\frac{3}{7}x - ay = b$$

In the system of equations above, a and b are constants. If the system has an infinite number of solutions, what is the value of b ?

A) 60

B) 1

C) $\dfrac{4}{15}$

D) $\dfrac{60}{7}$

Handedness	Grade	
	7th	8th
Right		
Left		
Total	322	356

The incomplete table above summarizes the number of right- and left-handed students by grade at Warren Junior High School. None of the students are both right- and left-handed. The ratio of right-handed 7th graders to left-handed 7th graders is 21 to 2. There are 4 more left-handed 8th graders than left-handed 7th graders. If an 8th grade student is chosen at random, what is the probability that the student is right-handed?

A) 9.0%

B) 52.4%

C) 91.0%

D) 92.1%

> a is five more than half of b.
>
> b minus c is three less than a.
>
> c is two times d.

For constants a, b, c, and d, the statements above are true. Which of the following must also be true?

A) $b - 2d = \frac{1}{2}b + 2$

B) $b - 2d - 3 = a$

C) $b - c - 8 = \frac{1}{2}b$

D) $b + c = a - 17$

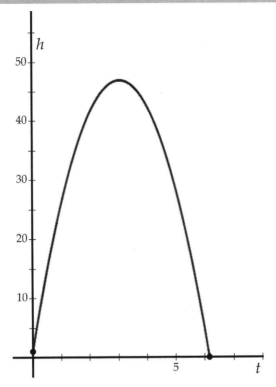

The graph above represents the height, h, in meters of a baseball as a function of time, t, in seconds. At time $t = 0$, the baseball is hit in the air. Which of the following equations best matches the flight of the baseball?

A) $h = -4.9t^2 - 30t - 1$

B) $h = 4.9t^2 - 30t - 1$

C) $h = 4.9t^2 + 30t + 1$

D) $h = -4.9t^2 + 30t + 1$

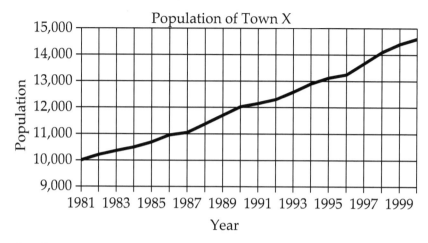

The chart above shows the population of Town X over two decades, from 1981 to 2000. A demographer estimates that the town's population has increased by about 2% per year. If x is the number of years after 1981, which of the following functions P best models the data?

A) $P(x) = 0.02x + 10{,}000$

B) $P(x) = 10{,}000 \times 0.02^x$

C) $P(x) = 10{,}000 \times 1.02^x$

D) $P(x) = 10{,}000x^{1.02}$

> a is greater than b.
>
> The sum of a and b is 11.
>
> The difference between a and b is 8.

For positive constants a and b, the above statements are true. What is the value of $a^2 - b^2$?

Level 2

If the equation $x^2 + y^2 - 10x + 14y = -70$ is graphed in the xy-plane, it forms a circle. What is the radius of the circle?

In the equation below, a is a positive integer constant.

$$y = -(x-a)^2 + 9$$

When the equation is graphed in the xy-plane, one of the graph's x-intercepts is at $x = 8$. What is the least possible value of a?

In the xy-plane, the point $(k, 5)$, where k is a constant, lies on the graph of the function f, which is defined as $f(x) = x^2 - 13x + 35$. What is one possible value of k?

$$P = 5w + \frac{2}{3}t + \frac{3}{10}m$$

Speedy Courier Service delivers packages by car. The service uses the equation above to calculate P, the total fee in dollars to deliver a package. In the equation, w is the weight of the package in pounds, t is the amount of driving time in minutes required to deliver the package, and m is the number of miles the courier must drive to deliver the package. A customer has a 3-pound package that she needs delivered to a colleague 30 miles away. If the delivery fee is $54, what is the driver's average speed in miles per hour?

A)   30 miles per hour

B)   40 miles per hour

C)   45 miles per hour

D)   55 miles per hour

A parabola with equation $y = (x - p)(x - 5)$, where p is a constant, is graphed in the xy-plane. The x-coordinate of the vertex of the parabola is 9. What is the value of p ?

A) −18

B) −4

C) 4

D) 13

In the xy-plane, line m passes through the origin. Which of the following sets of ordered pairs could be on line m ?

A) $(8, 5)$ and $(13, 10)$

B) $\left(-\dfrac{1}{3}, 3\right)$ and $\left(\dfrac{1}{9}, -1\right)$

C) $\left(2, \dfrac{1}{2}\right)$ and $\left(-\dfrac{1}{2}, -2\right)$

D) $(5, 4)$ and $(25, 16)$

48.
Level 3

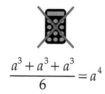

$$\frac{a^3 + a^3 + a^3}{6} = a^4$$

What positive value of a satisfies the equation above?

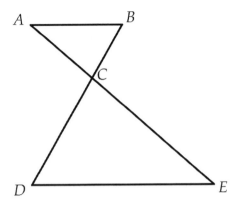

In the figure above, $\overline{AB} \parallel \overline{DE}$. If $AB = 5$, $DE = 10$, and $BC = \dfrac{10}{3}$, what is the length of $\overline{BD}$?

A) $\dfrac{20}{9}$

B) $\dfrac{20}{3}$

C) 10

D) 15

$$3x^2 + bx + 24 = (3x + 8)(x + a)$$

If the equation above is true for all values of x, what is the value of b?

A machine at a factory that makes phonograph records ensures that each disc produced has a mass between 198 and 212 grams, inclusive, by rejecting discs with masses outside that range. Which of the following inequalities represents the full range of disc masses, m, that the machine will not reject?

A) $|m - 205| \leq 7$

B) $|m - 205| \leq 14$

C) $|m - 198| \leq 14$

D) $|m - 212| \leq 14$

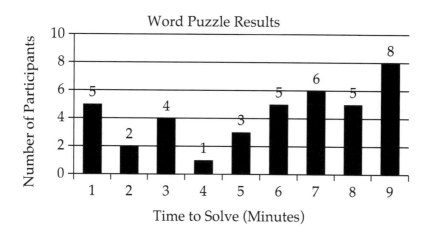

Word Puzzle Results

The frequency graph above represents the time, in minutes, it took 39 people to complete a word puzzle. What is the median number of minutes it took for members of this group to complete the puzzle?

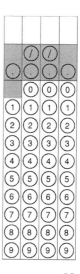

If $f(x+7) = 5x+5$ for all values of x, which of the following is equal to $f(2x)$?

A) $10x+19$

B) $10x+14$

C) $10x-30$

D) $10x-60$

Mr. Mehta's Math Classes	
Class	Enrollment
A	27
B	34
C	33

The table above shows the number of students in three 11th grade math classes taught by Mr. Mehta at South High School. The ratio of boys to girls in Class A is 5 to 4. The ratio of boys to girls in Class B is 1 to 1. The ratio of boys to girls in Class C is 4 to 7. How many more girls than boys does Mr. Mehta teach in his three 11th grade math classes?

What value of x satisfies the equation $\dfrac{\left(3^x\right)^2}{3^{3x}} = \dfrac{1}{27}$?

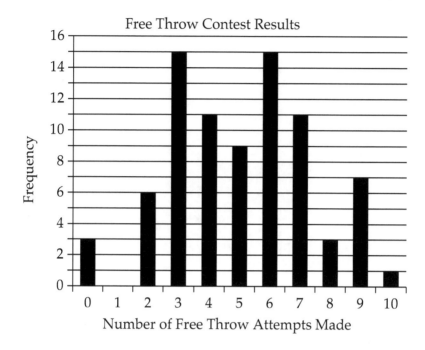

Free Throw Contest Results

The histogram above shows the results of a free throw contest held at the grand opening of a new sporting goods store. 81 people participated in the contest; each participant attempted 10 free throws. What was the median number of free throw attempts made?

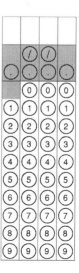

A certain polygon has n sides; each side has a length of 7 inches. Each interior angle in the polygon measures 162°. What is the perimeter of the polygon?

A)   98 inches

B)   119 inches

C)   128 inches

D)   140 inches

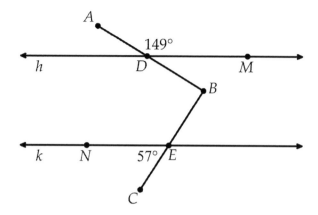

In the figure above, the measure of ∠ADM is 149°, the measure of ∠CEN is 57°, and lines h and k are parallel. What is the measure of ∠ABC ?

A) 98°

B) 92°

C) 88°

D) 82°

If $2^a + 2^a = 2^{b+3}$, what is the value of $a - b$?

A) 1

B) 2

C) 3

D) 5

$$f(x) = \frac{3x^2 + 4x + 18}{x^2 - ax + 11}$$

In the rational function above, a is a constant. The function is defined for all but two values of x. If one of the values of x for which the function is undefined is 1, what is the value of a?

$$2y + 3 > x - 2$$
$$y - 8 < 2x - 5$$

Which of the following ordered pairs (x, y) is in the solution set of the system of inequalities above?

A) $(-3, -1)$

B) $(-1, -4)$

C) $(4, -1)$

D) $(2, 5)$

62.
Level 3

The average age of all the people in a pre-kindergarten classroom, 17 children and two adults, is eight years. When one of the adults leaves the room temporarily, the average age in the room becomes six years. What is the age, in years, of the adult who left the room?

If $f(x+3) = 3x+1$ for all values of x, what is the value of $f(10)$?

Which of the following expressions is equivalent to $\dfrac{8x+4}{2x+8}$?

A) $x + \dfrac{2}{x}$

B) $4x + \dfrac{1}{2}$

C) $4 - \dfrac{14}{x+4}$

D) $4 + \dfrac{7}{x+4}$

$$3x - \frac{1}{3}y = a$$

$$ax - y = 27$$

In the system of equations above, a is a constant. For what value of a will the system have an infinite number of solutions?

$$3x + y = 11$$

$$10x - 2y = 2$$

The system of equations above has solution (x, y). What is the value of xy ?

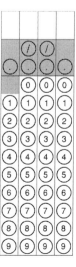

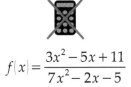

$$f(x) = \frac{3x^2 - 5x + 11}{7x^2 - 2x - 5}$$

The values a and b are not included in the domain of the rational function above. What is the value of $a + b$?

What is the greater of the two x-intercepts of the parabola with the equation $y = -(x-7)^2 + 4$?

Team 1 Individual Scores	Player 1	Player 2	Player 3	Player 4	Player 5
	63	44	34	33	50

Team 2 Individual Scores	Player 6	Player 7	Player 8	Player 9	Player 10
	47	66	47	31	

In a certain game, two teams with five members each compete for the highest team score. A team's score is determined by eliminating the team's greatest and least individual scores and then calculating the average (arithmetic mean) of the remaining three individual scores. The individual scores of nine of the ten players in a game are shown in the table above. What is the lowest integer score Player 10 can have so that Team 2 wins the game?

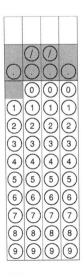

What is the solution set of the equation $5 - x = \sqrt{x - 3}$?

A) {4}

B) {3, 5}

C) {4, 7}

D) {3, 7}

What is the radius of the circle formed by the equation
$x^2 + y^2 + 10x + 2y = 64$?

A) $\sqrt{38}$

B) 8

C) $3\sqrt{10}$

D) 90

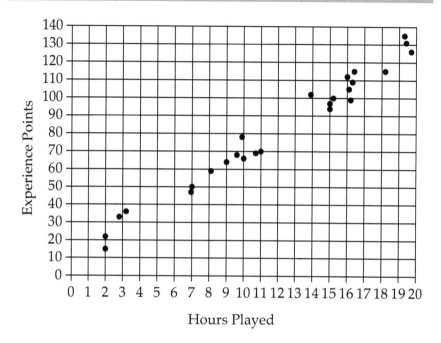

The scatterplot above represents a sample of players of an online video game. The number of hours each player has played (h) is plotted on the horizontal axis and the number of experience points each player has collected (p) is plotted on the vertical axis. Which of the following could be the equation of the line of best fit for this data?

A) $p = 0.5t + 10$

B) $p = t + 12$

C) $p = 6t + 9$

D) $p = 10t + 5$

$$(2x - a)^2 = 4x^2 - bx + a + 12$$

In the equation above, a and b are positive constants. If the equation is true for all values of x, what is the value of a ?

A company is forming a task force to brainstorm ways to improve its revenues. 30% of those invited to join the task force are sales people, 15% are marketing personnel, and 40% are product designers. The 3 remaining members of the task force are executives. If the task force were to be expanded to include 2 more product designers, then product designers would make up approximately what percent of the task force?

A) 42%

B) 44%

C) 45%

D) 50%

$$(x + a)(2x - b) = ax^2 + (2a - b)x - 32$$

If the above equation is true for all values of x, what is the value of b ?

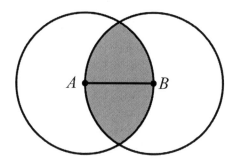

The figure above shows two circles with centers at points A and B. If the length of $\overline{AB}$ is 8 inches, what is the perimeter of the shaded region, in inches?

A) 8π

B) $\dfrac{24\pi}{5}$

C) $\dfrac{32\pi}{3}$

D) 16π

Which of the following equations, when graphed, does not contain any points in Quadrant IV?

A) $y = |3 - x| - 1$

B) $y = |x - 1| - 3$

C) $y = 1 - |3 - x|$

D) $y = |3 + x| - 1$

$$\frac{1}{5}x + \frac{3}{4}y = 3$$

$$x - 15y = 5$$

What value of x satisfies the system of equations above?

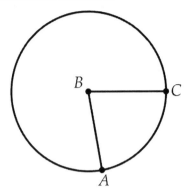

In the figure above, *B* is the center of the circle and points *A* and *C* are on the circle. If *AB* = 45 cm and the length of minor arc *AC* is 20π cm, what is the measure, in degrees, of $\angle ABC$? (Disregard the degree symbol when entering your answer.)

The circle with equation $(x-3)^2+(y+4)^2=9$ is plotted in the xy-plane. Which of the following ordered pairs (x, y) represents a point on the circle?

A) $(0, 4)$

B) $\left(-3-\dfrac{3\sqrt{2}}{2}, 4+\dfrac{3\sqrt{2}}{2}\right)$

C) $(6, -1)$

D) $\left(\dfrac{3}{2}, \dfrac{3\sqrt{3}}{2}-4\right)$

A square is formed in the xy-plane by connecting four points: $(1, -2)$, $(2, 3)$, $(7, 2)$, and (a, b), where a and b are constants. What is the value of $a - b$?

$$y = 3x + 4$$
$$ax - by = 11$$

In the system of equations above, a and b are constants. If the system has no solutions, what is the value of $\dfrac{b}{a}$?

A) $-\dfrac{1}{3}$

B) $\dfrac{1}{3}$

C) $\dfrac{11}{3}$

D) 3

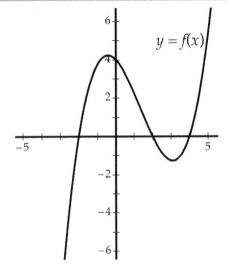

The figure above shows the graph of the polynomial function $y = f(x)$ in the xy-plane. Which of the following points is NOT on the graph of $y = -2f(x)$?

A) $(0, -8)$

B) $(-4, 0)$

C) $(2, 0)$

D) $(4, 0)$

In the xy-plane, the line $y = 8$ intersects a certain parabola exactly once. Which of the following could be the equation of the parabola?

A) $y = \dfrac{1}{8}(x - 8)(x + 8)$

B) $y = -\dfrac{1}{8}(x - 8)(x + 8)$

C) $y = (x + 8)(8 - x)$

D) $y = (x - 8)(8 - x)$

In the equation below, a is a constant.

$$y = 3(x - a)(x + 6)$$

When the equation above is graphed in the xy-plane, it forms a parabola with a vertex at $(-2, -48)$. What is the value of a ?

Both Louis and Marcy work at jobs where they can collect overtime pay at a rate of 150% of their regular hourly wages for each hour they work beyond 40 hours in a week. Marcy's regular pay rate is $18 per hour, and Louis's regular pay rate is $16 per hour. Last week, Marcy worked for 48 hours and Louis made $64 more than Marcy. How many hours did Louis work last week?

In the equations below, a is a constant.

$$4x + 7y = 30$$

$$ax - 2y = 5$$

If the equations above are graphed in the xy-plane, they form perpendicular lines. What is the value of a ?

88.
Level 4

Triangle ABC has a perimeter of 150 inches. The measure of angle A is 90°, and $\sin B = \dfrac{5}{13}$. What is the length of $\overline{AB}$, in inches?

A) 12

B) 23

C) 60

D) 65

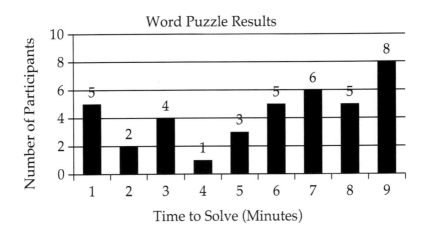

The frequency graph above represents the time, in minutes, it took 39 people to complete a word puzzle. Which of the following box plots accurately represents the same data?

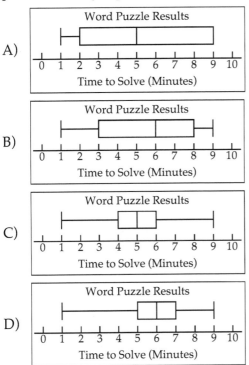

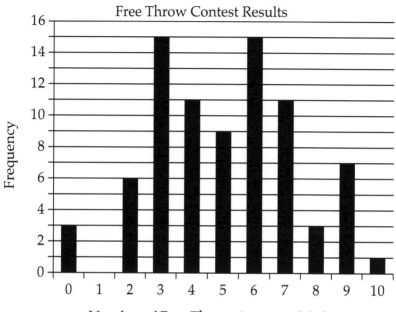

Free Throw Contest Results

Number of Free Throw Attempts Made

The histogram above shows the results of a free throw contest held at the grand opening of a new sporting goods store. 81 people participated in the contest; each participant attempted 10 free throws. If 9 more people had entered the contest and each of them made 5 out of 10 free throws, how would the standard deviation of the data be different?

A) The standard deviation would be higher.

B) The standard deviation would be lower.

C) The standard deviation would not be different.

D) It cannot be determined from the information given.

A fish tank at a pet store contains red and blue fish. The ratio of red fish to blue fish is 4 to 7. After a customer purchases 5 blue fish from the tank, the ratio of red fish to blue fish becomes 3 to 4. How many red fish are in the tank?

In triangle ABC, the measure of $\angle B$ is 90° and $\cos(\angle A) = \dfrac{5}{13}$. If $AB = 60$, what is the value of BC ?

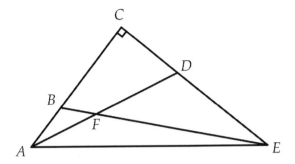

In the figure above, the measure of ∠CAD is 26° and the measure of ∠BEC is 28°. What is the measure of ∠BFD in degrees? (Disregard the ° sign when gridding your answer.)

Which of the following equations, when plotted in the xy-plane, will create a line that passes through the point $(2, 5)$ and is parallel to the line formed by $3x - 4y = 12$?

A) $-6x + 8y = 28$

B) $3x - 4y = -12$

C) $-3x + 4y = -14$

D) $-6x - 8y = -52$

In the equation below, a, b, and c are constants.

$$ax^2 + 3x - b = (2x + 5)(3x - c)$$

If the equation is true for all values of x, what is the value of abc ?

In the xy-plane, line m has the equation $y = -5x + a$, where a is a constant. Line n passes through the origin and is perpendicular to line m. If line m and line n intersect at the point $(15, b)$, where b is a constant, what is the value of a ?

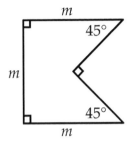

The area of the figure above is 108 square inches. What is the value of m, in inches?

In the equation below, the angle measures are in radians and a is a constant.

$$\sin\left(\frac{\pi}{8}\right) = \cos\left(\frac{\pi}{a}\right)$$

Which of the following could be the value of a ?

A) 8

B) $\dfrac{8}{3}$

C) $\dfrac{8}{7}$

D) $\dfrac{7}{8}$

$$y = 3x + 3a$$

$$y = ax + 9$$

In the system of equations above, a is a constant. If the equations are graphed in the xy-plane, they form perpendicular lines. At what point do the lines intersect?

A) $(3, 10)$

B) $(10, 3)$

C) $(3, 0)$

D) $(3, 8)$

$$\frac{2x+10}{x^2-x-6}=\frac{x+3}{x-3}$$

What is the solution set of the equation above?

A) $\{-4\}$

B) $\{-4, 1\}$

C) $\{-4, 2\}$

D) $\{2, 3\}$

$$y = x^2 + x - 8$$
$$y = 2x - 2$$

If (x, y) is a solution to the system of equations above, what is the greatest possible value of $|x - y|$?

A) 1

B) 4

C) 7

D) 8

$$y = 5$$

$$y = a(x - b)^2 + c$$

In the system of equations above, a, b, and c are constants. For which of the following values of a, b, and c does the system have no solutions?

A) $a = -2, b = 1, c = 7$

B) $a = 3, b = 1, c = -3$

C) $a = 6, b = -3, c = 2$

D) $a = -5, b = 5, c = 4$

x	$f(x)$
0	24
6	22
15	19

Some values of the linear function f are given in the table above. If $g(x) = 3f(x)$, what is the value of $g(8)$?

$$\frac{\left(\frac{x^a x^2}{x^3}\right)^3}{x^a} = x^5$$

In the equation above, a is a constant. What is the value of a?

Christine is taking a timed math test with 30 questions. She is allowed to spend 50 minutes on the test. She spends an average of 50 seconds per question on the first 8 questions. She spends an average of 134 seconds per question on the next 15 questions. If she wants to have 5 minutes left after she completes all 30 questions so that she can check her work, what must be her average time, in seconds, for the final 7 questions? Round your answer to the nearest second.

In the *xy*-plane, a triangle is formed with vertices at (5, 3), (–2 , –2), and (0, –2). What is the area of the triangle?

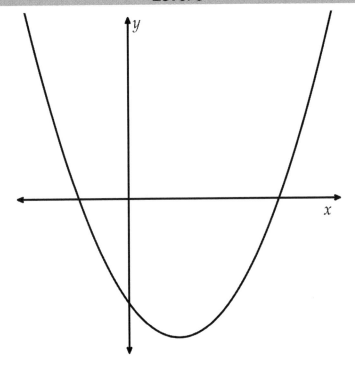

The figure above shows the graph of $y = a(x + b)(x + c)$, where a, b, and c are constants and $|c| > |b|$. Which of the following must be true?

    I. $a > 0$

    II. $c > b$

    III. $bc < 0$

A) I only

B) II only

C) I, II, and III

D) I and III only

$$3x + 4y = 8$$
$$2x + 8y = 4$$
$$10x - ay = a$$

If the three equations above are graphed in the xy-plane, they form three lines that intersect at one point. What is the value of the constant a ?

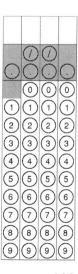

Which of the following inequalities has as its solution set all points that are a distance of 4 or less from –5 ?

A) $|x + 4| \leq -5$

B) $|x - 5| \leq 4$

C) $|x + 5| \leq 4$

D) $|x - 4| \geq -5$

$$8x + 3y = 37$$
$$5y = 4x - 12$$

What value of y satisfies the system of equations above?

If $\sin x° = \cos y°$, $0 < x < y < 90$, and $xy = 800$, what is the value of $x^2 + y^2$?

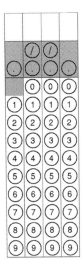

A musician recorded 15 songs with an average length of 215 seconds for potential inclusion on his new album. After discussion with the label that would release the album, it was decided that the final version of the album would include 13 songs and have a duration of 48 minutes and 15 seconds. No silence was added between songs. What is the average length, in seconds, of the recorded songs that were EXCLUDED from the final version of the album?

$$x^2 + y^2 + ax + by = c$$

In the equation above, a, b, and c are constants. If the equation represents a circle with center $(5, -2)$ and radius 7, what is the value of c?

If $ab = 19$ and $a - b = 7$, what is the value of $a^2 + b^2$?

Height of Water in Tank over Time

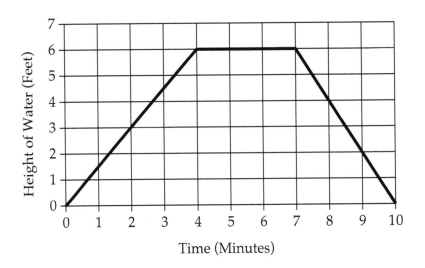

Time (Minutes)

The graph above shows the height, in feet, of water in a tank over a particular ten minute period. At the beginning of the ten minutes, a hose at the top of the tank was turned on. Four minutes later, the hose was turned off. Three minutes after that, a drain at the bottom of the tank was opened.

On a different day, the same tank is filled with water to a height of four feet. Then, a student opens the drain, turns on the hose, and begins a timer simultaneously. How much time elapses before the tank is empty?

A) Three minutes

B) Four minutes

C) Six minutes

D) Eight minutes

Valentina is shopping for apartments. She sees one advertisement for an apartment on Maple Street that has a total area of 715 square feet and another advertisement for an apartment on Elm Street that has an area of 200 square meters. Which of the following statements is true? (Note: 1 foot = 0.3048 meters)

A) The area of the apartment on Maple Street is about 3 times that of the apartment on Elm Street.

B) The area of the apartment on Maple street is about 9 percent greater than that of the apartment on Elm Street.

C) The area of the apartment on Maple Street is about 8 percent less than that of the apartment on Elm Street.

D) The area of the apartment on Maple Street is about $\frac{1}{3}$ of that of the apartment on Elm Street.

The product of the complex numbers $5 - 7i$ and $a + bi$, where a and b are constants, is 148. What is the sum of a and b ? (Note: $i = \sqrt{-1}$)

$$y > \frac{1}{3}x - 3$$

$$y > 2x + 1$$

If the system of inequalities above is graphed in the xy-plane and the ordered pair (a, b) is in the solution set, then which of the following statements cannot be disproven?

A) If $a > 0$, then $b > 0$.

B) If $a < 0$, then $b < 0$.

C) If $a < 0$, then $b > 0$.

D) If $a > 0$, then $b < 0$.

In the xy-plane, the graph of $y = f(x)$ is a line. If $f(3) = 8$ and $f(8) = 3$, which of the following is true?

A) $f(f(4)) = 4$

B) $f(0) = f(11)$

C) $f(-3) = -8$

D) $f(10) = -1$

Level 5

$$y \le (x - 3)^2$$
$$y \ge -x + 9$$

In the xy-plane, a point with coordinates (a, b) lies in the solution set of the system of inequalities above. If a and b are greater than zero, what is the least possible value of a ?

The expression $4(x-5)(x+6)+m$, where m is a constant, can be rewritten as a binomial square in the form of $(ax+b)^2$, where a and b are integer constants. What is the value of m ?

x	$f(x)$
0	15
1	0
2	-7
3	0
4	27
5	80

The table above shows some values of the polynomial function f. Which of the following is a factor of $f(x+3)$?

A) x

B) $x-1$

C) $x-2$

D) $x+3$

Which of the following statements CANNOT be true about a set of 10 numbers?

    I. The median of the 10 numbers is one of the 10 numbers.

    II. The sum of the 10 numbers is equal to the average (arithmetic mean) of the 10 numbers.

    III. The set of 10 numbers has 6 modes.

A) I and II

B) II and III

C) I, II, and III

D) III only

In the complex number system, $(4+7i)(a+bi)=130$ for some constants a and b. What is the value of $a + b$? (Note: $i = \sqrt{-1}$)

A) 22

B) 3

C) –3

D) –6

A cube with edges of length $6\sqrt{3}$ is inscribed in a sphere with volume $a\pi$. What is the value of a ?

(Note: The formula for the volume of a sphere is $V = \dfrac{4}{3}\pi r^3$.)

Solutions

Lines; Translating between Words and Math

Take this one step at a time. Here's the original line:

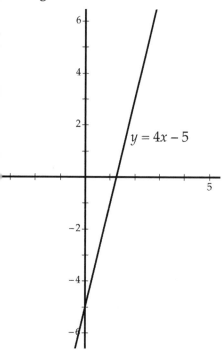

When we reflect a line across the x-axis, its slope and its y-intercept are negated. So the equation of the reflection is going to be $y = -4x+5$. Here's that one:

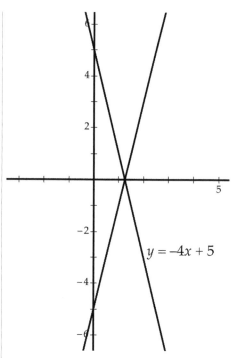

Now Heather needs to draw a line perpendicular to the reflection (in other words, perpendicular to the blue line above) that crosses it at its y-intercept. We know its slope will be $\frac{1}{4}$ because it's perpendicular to a line with a slope of -4, and we know its y-intercept will be 5 because that's where it meets the other line whose y-intercept we know. Here they all are together:

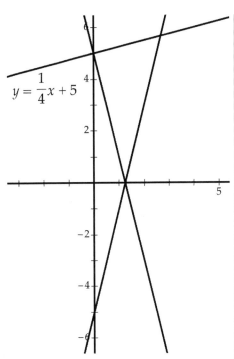

$$y = \frac{1}{4}x + 5$$

$$\frac{1}{3} + \frac{4}{2(3)} = \frac{27}{3(3)^2}$$

$$\frac{1}{3} + \frac{4}{6} = \frac{27}{27}$$

$$\frac{1}{3} + \frac{2}{3} = 1$$

Yup—that works!

---

3. D
Plugging In; Solving Systems of Linear Equations

We have a wealth of options here. First, we could plug in values for a and b. From there, we can graph or solve algebraically. For example, we could say $a = 2$ and $b = 17$; that would be consistent with the question's stipulation that $b = a + 15$. Then we could graph:

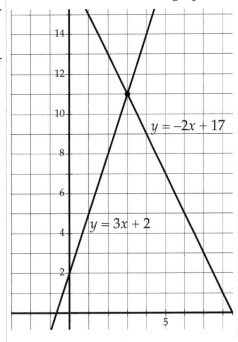

$$y = -2x + 17$$
$$y = 3x + 2$$

---

2. D
Backsolving; Algebraic Manipulation

To solve this algebraically, just multiply the equation by $3x^2$ to eliminate all the denominators, and then solve.

$$3x^2 \times \left(\frac{1}{x} + \frac{4}{2x}\right) = \left(\frac{27}{3x^2}\right) \times 3x^2$$

$$3x + 6x = 27$$

$$9x = 27$$

$$x = 3$$

Since this is a multiple choice question, we also have the wonderful option of backsolving. Just try each choice until one gives you a working equation. Here's how that looks with the right answer:

127

We don't even need to do any more to see that the answer must be $x = 3$.

A more algebraic way to go is to do some substitution. First, substitute $a + 15$ for b:

$y = 3x + a$

$y = -2x + a + 15$

Then, since both equations already have y isolated and we only care about x anyway, we can set the equations equal and solve:

$3x + a = -2x + a + 15$

$3x = -2x + 15$

$5x = 15$

$x = 3$

---

4. B
Plugging In; Exponents; Functions

This is a great opportunity to plug in. Let's say $b = 2$, which means $a = 2^6 = 64$.

To find $f(g(64))$, just work from the inside out!

$f(g(64))$

$f(\sqrt{64})$

$f(8)$

8^3

512

Now let's just see which answer choice gives us 512 when you plug in 2 for b! Only choice B works.

The algebraic solution isn't much worse—it just requires us to know the exponent rules.

$f(g(a))$

$= f(g(b^6))$

$= f(\sqrt{b^6})$

$= f(b^3)$

$= (b^3)^3$

$= b^9$

Of course, both of the solutions above require us to be comfortable with function notation!

---

5. C
Translating between Words and Math; Solving Systems of Linear Equations

To get this one, write and solve a system of linear equations. Say the fee for an adult is x and the fee for a child is y. Then you can say:

$3x + 5y = 70.5$

$2x + 6y = 67$

We can solve this system with multiple methods, but this time let's substitute after isolating x in the second equation.

$\dfrac{2x + 6y}{2} = \dfrac{67}{2}$

$x + 3y = 33.5$

$x = 33.5 - 3y$

$3(33.5 - 3y) + 5y = 70.5$

$100.5 - 9y + 5y = 70.5$

$30 - 4y = 0$

$30 = 4y$

$7.5 = y$

So it's $7.50 per child. To find the adult price, solve for x:

$$2x + 6(7.5) = 67$$

$$2x + 45 = 67$$

$$2x = 22$$

$$x = 11$$

Now that we know it's $11 per adult, we can finally calculate the cost for 2 children and 1 adult:

$$2(7.5) + 11 = 26$$

---

6. C
Parabolas

The equation we're given is in vertex form (that is, $y = a(x - h)^2 + k$ where (h , k) is the vertex of the parabola), so we know right away that $k = 16$. So let's rewrite the equation and put it in standard form:

$$y = -(x - 5)^2 + 16$$

$$y = -(x^2 - 10x + 25) + 16$$

$$y = -x^2 + 10x - 25 + 16$$

$$y = -x^2 + 10x - 9$$

Hmm...can we factor that? Remember, when a parabola is in factored form, it tells us the x-intercepts!

$$y = -x^2 + 10x - 9$$

$$y = -(x^2 - 10x + 9)$$

$$y = -(x - 1)(x - 9)$$

So the x-intercepts are 1 and 9, which means $a + b = 1 + 9 = 10$.

---

7. B
Right Triangles and Basic Trigonometry

First, let's draw the triangle—that will make it that much easier to SOH-CAH-TOA this question, and really, how long does it take to draw a *triangle*?

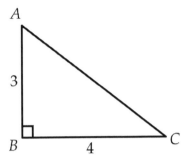

The tangent is the ratio of the opposite side to the adjacent leg, so we know that if $\tan A = \dfrac{4}{3}$, the sides labeled 3 and 4 are either exactly that, or some other values with that ratio. To make things easy on ourselves, let's just plug in 3 and 4.

From there, we have two paths. The first and more preferable is recognizing that $\dfrac{\sin C}{\cos C} = \tan C$. If we see that, then all we need to do is look at our diagram to see that $\tan C = \dfrac{3}{4}$.

The other, slightly longer path, is to recognize the 3-4-5 triangle, evaluate the sine and cosine separately, and then divide those values. That works well enough:

$$\frac{\sin C}{\cos C}$$

$$= \frac{\left(\dfrac{3}{5}\right)}{\left(\dfrac{4}{5}\right)}$$

$$= \frac{3}{5} \times \frac{5}{4}$$

$$= \frac{3}{4}$$

---

8. 0.8, 4/5
Right Triangles and Basic Trigonometry

To get this one, we need to recognize that triangles ABC and DEC are similar. We know this because they have vertical angles at point C, and they each have right angles as well: Angle-Angle similarity.

From there, knowing that $ED = 3$ and $AB = 6$ tells us that all the sides of triangle ABC are twice as long as their corresponding sides in triangle DEC.

We can use this fact to figure out the lengths of the other legs because we know their sum: $EB = 12$. If we say $EC = x$, then we must say $BC = 2x$. So we can solve:

$$12 = x + 2x$$

$$12 = 3x$$

$$4 = x$$

If $ED = 3$ and $EC = 4$, then triangle DEC is a 3-4-5 triangle—$CD = 5$.

Remember SOH-CAH-TOA: the sine of an angle is equal to the

length of its Opposite leg over the Hypotenuse.

Therefore, $\sin D = \dfrac{4}{5}$.

---

9. D
Solving Systems of Linear Equations

We're only being asked to find the value of x that satisfies the system. We don't care about y, so let's try to eliminate that quickly. If we multiply the second equation by 4, we'll be able to eliminate the y terms by adding the equations together!

$$4 \times (5x - y) = (3) \times 4$$

$$20x - 4y = 12$$

Add that the the first equation now:

$$x + 4y = n$$
$$\underline{+\ 20x - 4y = 12}$$
$$21x + 0y = n + 12$$

From there, we've got x alone as soon as we divide by 21.

$$21x = n + 12$$

$$x = \frac{n+12}{21}$$

---

10. B
Circles, Radians, and a Little More Trigonometry; Right Triangles and Basic Trigonometry

The thing to remember to get this one right is that tangent lines are perpendicular to the radii they connect with, so if we draw in segments *AM* and *BM*, we end up making a square.

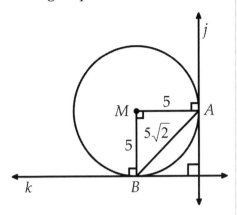

The chord $\overline{AB}$ is therefore the diagonal of a square, A.K.A. the hypotenuse of a 45°-45°-90° triangle. We're given that $AB = 5\sqrt{2}$, so we can conclude that *AM* and *BM*, the legs of the triangle, each equal 5. In other words, the radius of the circle is 5.

From there, it's easy to calculate the circumference:

$C = 2\pi r$

$C = 2\pi(5)$

$C = 10\pi$

---

11. 5
Exponents and Exponential Functions

Gotta know the exponent rules to get this one. First, remember that when we multiply two exponential expressions with the same base, we add the exponents. Thus:

$\left(x^{2y}\right)\left(x^{3y}\right) = \left(x^{y}\right)^{a}$

$x^{(2y+3y)} = \left(x^{y}\right)^{a}$

$x^{5y} = \left(x^{y}\right)^{a}$

From there, also remember that when we raise an exponential expression to a power, we multiply the exponents. Thus:

$x^{5y} = \left(x^{y}\right)^{a}$

$x^{5y} = x^{ay}$

If, as the question stipulates, *x* and *y* are greater than 1, the only way that equation is true is if $a = 5$.

---

12. B
Polynomials

While we *could* do this one with polynomial division, let's use multiplication instead. Multiply by the denominator to get rid of those ugly fractions!

$\dfrac{18x^2 + 15x - 12}{3x + 2} = 6x + 1 + \dfrac{a}{3x + 2}$

$18x^2 + 15x - 12 = (6x + 1)(3x + 2) + a$

$18x^2 + 15x - 12 = 18x^2 + 15x + 2 + a$

Now subtract out all the terms that match on both sides. We're left with simply –12 = 2 + *a*.

Solving that gives us –14 = *a*.

---

13. A
Plugging In; Parabolas; Binomial Squares and Difference of Two Squares

There are a few ways to go here, but the most universal might be to plug in some obvious points we can get from the graph. For example, we can see from the graph the the parabola goes through $(0, -3)$. Which of the given equations work with that?

Choice A does:

$$-3 = (0 + \sqrt{3})(0 - \sqrt{3})$$

$$-3 = (\sqrt{3})(-\sqrt{3})$$

$$-3 = -3$$

But none of the other choices do!

B:

$$-3 = (0 + 3)(0 - 3)$$

$$-3 \neq -9$$

C:

$$-3 = (0 - \sqrt{3})^2$$

$$-3 \neq 3$$

D:

$$-3 = (0 - 3)^2$$

$$-3 \neq 9$$

Another good way to go is recognize immediately that choice A is a difference of two squares that will resolve to $y = x^2 - 3$, which will be the classic $y = x^2$ parabola, just shifted down 3 units. That's definitely what the figure looks like!

---

14. A
Binomial Squares and Difference of Two Squares

Recognize the difference of two squares here? Anytime we see something in the form $a^2 - b^2$, it should be at the front of our minds that we can factor it to $(a + b)(a - b)$!

In this case, we treat $x^4 - y^4$ as a difference of two squares. (Really it's just the same as saying $(x^2)^2 - (y^2)^2$, which is *obviously* a difference of two squares.)

The algebra:

$$\frac{x^4 - y^4}{x^2 + y^2}$$

$$= \frac{(x^2 + y^2)(x^2 - y^2)}{x^2 + y^2}$$

$$= x^2 - y^2$$

Of course, we could keep factoring: $x^2 - y^2 = (x + y)(x - y)$. However, the answer choices don't require us to take that final step!

---

15. A
Algebraic Manipulation

We have two jobs here. First, we need to combine the given equations to come up with one equation that has everything we need in it—a formula for the density of a sphere. Once we've got that, we need to solve that equation for r.

Combining the equations is easy enough: V appears in both, so we can substitute.

$$p = \frac{m}{V} \qquad V = \frac{4}{3}\pi r^3$$

$$p = \frac{m}{\left(\frac{4}{3}\pi r^3\right)}$$

Now, just solve that for r. Step 1 is to take care of that nasty fraction-in-a-fraction. Remember: when we divide by a fraction, that's the same as multiplying by its reciprocal.

$$p = \frac{m}{\pi r^3} \times \frac{1}{\left(\dfrac{4}{3}\right)}$$

$$p = \frac{m}{\pi r^3} \times \frac{3}{4}$$

$$p = \frac{3m}{4\pi r^3}$$

Now multiply everything by r^3; we want to get r isolated so we might as well get it out of the denominator.

$$pr^3 = \frac{3m}{4\pi}$$

Keep isolating r—divide by p.

$$r^3 = \frac{3m}{4p\pi}$$

Now just take the cube root and we're done.

$$r = \sqrt[3]{\frac{3m}{4p\pi}}$$

16. B
Percents and Percent Change

This is a percent change question.

$$\% \text{ Change} = \frac{\text{Change}}{\text{Starting Value}} \times 100\%$$

The first task here is to figure out what the percent increase was from Monday to Tuesday. The increase was $16{,}830 - 15{,}300 = 1{,}530$, and the starting value was 15,300, so the percent change is:

$$\frac{1{,}530}{15{,}300} \times 100\% = 10\%$$

Now all we need to do is figure out what the value of the investment would be on Wednesday if it was a 10% decrease from Tuesday's value. To do that, we simply subtract 10% of 16,830 from 16,830:

$$16{,}830 - \frac{10}{100} \times 16{,}830 = 15{,}147$$

If the value of the investment at the end of the day Wednesday was $15,147, then it's easy enough to calculate how much less that is than the $15,300 on Monday: $15{,}300 - 15{,}147 = 153$. Therefore, the answer is B.

Shortcut for percent wizards:

$$15{,}300 - (15{,}300 \times 1.1 \times 0.9) = 153$$

17. C
Functions

The thing to recognize here is that if $g(x) = 2f(x) - 1$, then $g(1) = 2f(1) - 1$. Since we can find the value of $f(1)$ from the graph, the rest is just simple arithmetic.

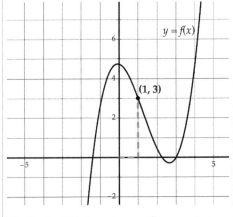

To find $f(1)$, just trace the x-axis to $x = 1$ and then trace straight up to the curve. The intersection of the curve and the $x = 1$ line will give us the value of $f(1)$.

Since the curve touches the $x = 1$ line at $(1, 3)$, we say that $f(1) = 3$. In fact, generally speaking we can say that if a point (a, b) lies on the graph of a function f, then $f(a) = b$.

Anyway, now that we have the value of $f(1)$, we can plug it into the expression we have for $g(1)$ to solve.

$$g(1) = 2f(1) - 1$$
$$g(1) = 2(3) - 1$$
$$g(1) = 5$$

---

18. 0.75, 3/4
Parabolas

When a question gives an equation with unknown constants and a point on its graph, *we plug the point into the equation*! We know the graph contains $(8, 8)$, so:

$$y = a(x - 6)^2 + 5$$
$$8 = a(8 - 6)^2 + 5$$
$$8 = a(2)^2 + 5$$
$$8 = 4a + 5$$
$$3 = 4a$$
$$\frac{3}{4} = a$$

I doubt many will prefer what I'm about to say to what I've already said, but another way to go here is to recognize that the equation you're given is in vertex form. If we recognize that, then we know that the vertex of this parabola is at $(6, 5)$. If a were equal to 1, then the parabola would move 2 to the right to an x-coordinate of 8 and move 4 up to a y-coordinate of 9. However, *this* parabola only moves up 3, which is 0.75 of the way there.

---

19. 3
Algebraic Manipulation

To get moving on this one, cross multiply to clear the fractions and FOIL.

$$\frac{x - 8}{x + 2} = \frac{x - 5}{x - 1}$$
$$(x - 8)(x - 1) = (x - 5)(x + 2)$$
$$x^2 - 9x + 8 = x^2 - 3x - 10$$

The x^2 terms conveniently cancel out, and we're left to solve a linear equation for x. How sweet is that?

$$-9x + 8 = -3x - 10$$
$$18 = 6x$$
$$3 = x$$

---

20. B
Translating between Words and Math; Polynomials

The first thing we need to do here is translate the words into math:

$$10x^2 + ax - 36 = (2x + b)(cx + 4)$$

From there, keeping in mind that corresponding coefficients of equivalent polynomials must be equal, we should be able to see that for FOILing to work, $2cx^2$ must equal $10x^2$, and $4b$ must equal -36. So we can conclude that $c = 5$ and $b = -9$.

Of course, we need the value for a, so we still have to FOIL with those values in there.

$$10x^2 + ax - 36 = (2x - 9)(5x + 4)$$

$$10x^2 + ax - 36 = 10x^2 - 37x - 36$$

There we have it: $a = -37$.

21. D
Polynomials

Remember that when we have equivalent polynomials, the corresponding coefficients in each polynomial will be equivalent. In other words, if

$ax^2 + bx + c = mx^2 + nx + p$ for all values of x, then $a = m$, $b = n$, and $c = p$.

The first thing to do to solve a question like this, then, is to get each side looking as similar as possible. In this case, that means FOILing on the left.

$$(3x + a)(4x + a) = 12x^2 + 28x + b$$

$$12x^2 + 3ax + 4ax + a^2 = 12x^2 + 28x + b$$

$$12x^2 + 7ax + a^2 = 12x^2 + 28x + b$$

From that, we have everything we need. Corresponding coefficients tell us that $7a = 28$ and $a^2 = b$.

$$7a = 28$$

$$a = 4$$

$$a^2 = b$$

$$4^2 = b$$

$$16 = b$$

22. B
Data Analysis 1; Percents and Percent Change

Only one of the choices will be true, so we just need to start working through choices until we find it. Pro tip: start with the fastest ones to check.

For example, C is easy to check--the range of passenger kilometers will be just the difference between the highest number and the lowest number: $5501 - 5100 = 401$, not 61, so C is not the answer.

D is pretty easy to check, too. The average passenger kilometers will be $\dfrac{5440 + 5469 + 5501 + 5320 + 5100}{5}$ which simplifies to 5366. That's closer to the 2009 number than the 2006 number, so D isn't true.

From there, B is probably easier to check than A. To calculate the percent decrease from 2009 to 2010, do the following:

$$\% \text{ Change} = \frac{\text{Change}}{\text{Starting Value}} \times 100\%$$

Passengers 2009-2010:

$$\frac{1374 - 1453}{1453} \times 100\% = -5.44\%$$

Passenger Miles 2009-2010:

$$\frac{5100 - 5320}{5320} \times 100\% = -4.14\%$$

So choice B is true: the percent decrease in passengers was greater than the percent decrease in passenger kilometers from 2009 to 2010.

(Just for good measure, A doesn't work. The median number of passengers per year is 1461 and the average is 1448. The average is less than the median.)

23. B
Complex Numbers

The only way to divide complex numbers like this is to multiply top and bottom by a clever form of one: the complex conjugate of the denominator divided by itself. In other words, our first step is this:

$$\frac{14-5i}{3-2i} \times \frac{3+2i}{3+2i}$$

This accomplishes the goal of making the denominator a real number, which allows us to divide. Just don't forget to substitute –1 whenever FOILing results in an i^2.

$$\frac{14-5i}{3-2i} \times \frac{3+2i}{3+2i}$$

$$= \frac{(14-5i)(3+2i)}{(3-2i)(3+2i)}$$

$$= \frac{42+28i-15i-10i^2}{9+6i-6i-4i^2}$$

$$= \frac{42+13i-10(-1)}{9-4(-1)}$$

$$= \frac{52+13i}{13}$$

$$= 4+i$$

4. A
acksolving; Translating etween Words and Math

his is a great question to acksolve. Start by assuming

choice C is correct and she sold 129 hamburgers. At $8 per hamburger, she'll have made $1,032 in burgers. She sells $\frac{2}{3}$ as many orders of fries, so she will have sold 86 orders of fries. At $5 per order, that's $430 for fries. Total sales: $1,032 + 430 = $1,462. That's not enough money, so she needs to sell more burgers.

Now try choice B, which says she sold 144 burgers. $\frac{2}{3}$ of that is 96, so she will have sold 96 orders of fries. Total sales: $144(8) + 96(5) = $1,632. That's warmer, but we're still not there. At this point, if we're in a real rush, we can just pick A, but if we have the time it shouldn't take long to confirm.

If she sold 153 burgers, then she sold $\frac{2}{3}(153) = 102$ orders of fries. $153(8) + 102(5) = $1,734. Done.

The algebra:

$$1,734 = 8x + 5\left(\frac{2}{3}x\right)$$

$$1,734 = 8x + \frac{10}{3}x$$

$$1,734 = \frac{34}{3}x$$

$$153 = x$$

25. 100
Binomial Squares and Difference of Two Squares

The fastest, most awesome way to get this question is to recognize that we've got difference-of-two-squares form here. Despite the presence of radicals, what we're given fits the $(a + b)(a - b) = a^2 - b^2$ form. Which is to say that we can solve thusly:

$(\sqrt{x} + 9)(\sqrt{x} - 9) = 19$

$(\sqrt{x})^2 - 81 = 19$

$x - 81 = 19$

$x = 100$

Easy, right?

26. B
Functions

For a question like this, all we have to do is take the full argument, $(x + 2)$, and put it everywhere an x used to be. Here's the algebra:

$f(x) = 2x^2 - 4x + 8$

$f(x + 2) = 2(x + 2)^2 - 4(x + 2) + 8$

$f(x + 2) = 2(x^2 + 4x + 4) - 4x - 8 + 8$

$f(x + 2) = 2x^2 + 8x + 8 - 4x$

$f(x + 2) = 2x^2 + 4x + 8$

27. 6
Binomial Squares and Difference of Two Squares

We *could* expand this all the way out, simplify it, and then factor or use the quadratic formula to solve. But since we're here honing our skills to PWN the SAT, let's solve this one the fast way. We can factor the given equation without expanding it first. To make that easier to see, let's temporarily replace $(x - 3)$ with a:

$0 = a^2 - 6a + 9$

That's an obvious binomial square —easy to factor!

$0 = (a - 3)^2$

All we need to do now is remember that $a = x - 3$ and substitute back in:

$0 = ((x - 3) - 3)^2$

$0 = (x - 6)^2$

So the value of x that satisfies the equation is 6.

28. A
Percents and Percent Change

The population grew by 3.2% from 2013 to 2014, then by 2.8% from 2014 to 2015, then by 2.6% from 2015 to 2016. To figure out what the 2016 population might be, we need to start with the population we know from 2013 and grow it incrementally by each of those percentages.

2014: $1{,}059{,}382 \times 1.032 \approx 1{,}093{,}282$

2015: $1{,}093{,}282 \times 1.028 \approx 1{,}123{,}894$

2016: $1{,}123{,}894 \times 1.026 \approx 1{,}153{,}115$

Choice A is the closest to 1,153,115, so that's the answer.

Note this a useful shortcut: you can just apply all those growth rates in one calculation:

$$\begin{aligned}
& 1{,}059{,}382 \\
\times\ & 1.032 \\
\times\ & 1.028 \\
\times\ & 1.026 \\
\approx\ & 1{,}153{,}115
\end{aligned}$$

29. D
Complex Numbers

To divide complex numbers, we must multiply by a clever form of one made up of the complex conjugate of the denominator. This makes the denominator a real number, and then we can just do normal division. In this case, that means we multiply our fraction by $\frac{8-i}{8-i}$:

$$\frac{26-13i}{8+i} \times \frac{8-i}{8-i}$$

$$= \frac{208 - 26i - 104i + 13i^2}{64 - i^2}$$

$$= \frac{208 - 130i + 13(-1)}{64 - (-1)}$$

$$= \frac{195 - 130i}{65}$$

$$= 3 - 2i$$

30. 9
Binomial Squares and Difference of Two Squares

Trying to solve for a and b directly here could lead to trouble—they aren't integers. Good thing we don't need to solve for them!

Note that the two equations we're given provide values for the pieces of the binomial square we're meant to find the value of! FOILing out $(a-b)^2$ gives us $a^2 - 2ab + b^2$, which of course can be rearranged to $a^2 + b^2 - 2ab$. We can substitute values right into there.

$$a^2 + b^2 - 2ab$$

$$= 19 - 2(5)$$

$$= 9$$

31. C
Data Analysis 1

Remember that the graph shows the cumulative total number of miles driven by the car, so the month during which Gerald drove the least miles will be the month that shows the smallest increase in height from the month prior. Visually, it should be fairly obvious that the bar for Month 3 is only very slightly taller than the bar for Month 2. What that means is that on the last day of Month 3, the odometer increased from the last day of Month 2 by a relatively small amount. Since no other month-to-month increase is smaller, the answer is Month 3.

32. A
Parabolas

This is a question about parabola symmetry—to get it, we need to remember that parabolas are symmetrical about the vertical line through their vertices. That means that the x-intercepts of the parabola will be equidistant from the $x = -4$ vertical line.

Since the point $(4, 0)$ is 8 units to the right of the $x = -4$ line, the other x-intercept is going to be 8 units to the left of the $x = -4$ line at $(-12, 0)$. Therefore, $a = -12$.

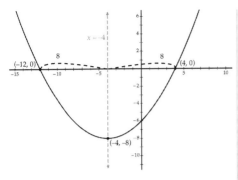

33. A
Exponents and Exponential Functions; Binomial Squares and Difference of Two Squares

To get this one, we need to remember the exponent rules. Specifically, that $c^a c^b$ simplifies to c^{a+b} and that $\dfrac{c^a}{c^b}$ simplifies to c^{a-b}. Once we've got those, we're off to the races.

If $c^{a+b} = c^{12}$, then $a + b = 12$.

If $c^{a-b} = c^3$, then $a - b = 3$.

We should also recognize the difference of two squares in the expression we're trying to match: $c^{a^2 - b^2}$ can be rewritten $c^{(a+b)(a-b)}$.

Once we see that, we're basically done. Just substitute!

$$c^{(a+b)(a-b)} = c^{(12)(3)} = c^{36}$$

34. B
Parabolas; Angles, Triangles, and Polygons

The vertex of that parabola will be at $(0, 4)$. The x-intercepts (points A and B) are at $(-2, 0)$ and $(2, 0)$. Therefore, the height of triangle

ABC will be 4, and its base will be 4. The area of the triangle will be equal to $\dfrac{1}{2}(4)(4) = 8$.

There are a number of ways to find the points we need in this question. One is just to be familiar enough with the structure of a parabola equation in standard form to recognize instantly that the parabola opens down from a vertex at $(0, 4)$ and will only travel left or right 2 units before it travels down 4 units to the x-axis.

To calculate those points algebraically (if desired), set y equal to zero and solve for the x-intercepts:

$$0 = x^2 - 4$$
$$0 = (x + 2)(x - 2)$$

Finally, we could just graph!

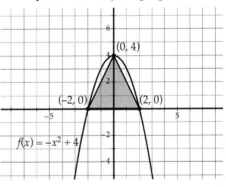

35. B
Exponents and Exponential Functions

Remember, when dividing the same base with different exponents, we subtract the exponents. Like so:

$$\frac{2^{a-b}}{2^{b-a}} = 4^c$$

$$2^{a-b-(b-a)} = 4^c$$

$$2^{2a-2b}$$

Let's go a few more steps, this time remembering that $4 = 2^2$, and that a power raised to a power means we multiply the powers.

$$2^{2(a-b)} = \left(2^2\right)^c$$

$$2^{2(a-b)} = 2^{2c}$$

From there, we can conclude that $2(a-b) = 2c$ and solve for b:

$$2(a-b) = 2c$$

$$a - b = c$$

$$-b = c - a$$

$$b = a - c$$

---

36. D
Lines; Solving Systems of Linear Equations

For a system of linear equations to have an infinite number of solutions, both equations must end up making the same line. In other words, both equations must have the same slope and the same y-intercept. So let's get the first equation into $y = mx + b$ form. First, let's multiply everything by 15 to make life easier:

$$5 \times \left(\frac{1}{5}x - \frac{1}{15}y\right) = (4) \times 15$$

$$x - y = 60$$

$$y = -3x + 60$$

$$= 3x - 60$$

Now, let's get the second equation into the same slope-intercept form:

$$\frac{3}{7}x - ay = b$$

$$-ay = -\frac{3}{7}x + b$$

$$y = \frac{3}{7a}x - \frac{b}{a}$$

For the system to have an infinite number of solutions, then, $\frac{3}{7a}$ must equal 3, and $-\frac{b}{a}$ must equal -60.

Solve for a:

$$\frac{3}{7a} = 3$$

$$3 = 21a$$

$$\frac{1}{7} = a$$

Then solve for b:

$$-\frac{b}{a} = -60$$

$$-\frac{b}{\left(\frac{1}{7}\right)} = -60$$

$$b = 60\left(\frac{1}{7}\right)$$

$$b = \frac{60}{7}$$

---

37. C
Ratios and Proportionality

The first thing we'll want to do here is fill in the table with unknowns so that we can solve. Because we're told that left-handed to right-handed 7th grade students are in a 2 to 21 ratio, let's put a $21x$ and a $2x$ in the 7th grade column.

	Grade	
Handedness	7th	8th
Right	$21x$	
Left	$2x$	
Total	322	356

Now we can solve for x—just remember that we don't actually care about x except that it will help us find $2x$ and $21x$!

$2x + 21x = 322$

$23x = 322$

$x = 14$

If $x = 14$, then $2x = 28$ and $21x = 294$, so let's put those in the table.

	Grade	
Handedness	7th	8th
Right	294	
Left	28	
Total	322	356

Now remember that there are 4 more left-handed 8th graders than left-handed 7th graders. If there are 28 left-handed 7th graders, then there must be 32 lefty 8th graders. Since the table tells us there are 356 total 8th graders, we know there are 356 – 32 = 324 right-handed 8th graders.

	Grade	
Handedness	7th	8th
Right	294	324
Left	28	32
Total	322	356

Now, let's choose an 8th grader at random. There are 356 8th graders to choose from, and 324 of them are right-handed. Therefore, the probability of our random 8th grader being right-handed is $\frac{324}{356} = 0.910112 \ldots$, or 91.0%.

---

38. A
Translating between Words and Math; Plugging In

Our first job here is to translate the statements into math sentences. Remember that "is" always means the equals sign!

a is five more than half of b:

$a = \frac{1}{2}b + 5$

b minus c is three less than a:
$b - c = a - 3$

c is two times d: $c = 2d$

From there, look for obvious substitutions in the answer choices. Choice A is the right answer because it makes two such "obvious" substitutions: into the second equation, $b - c = a - 3$, $2d$ is substituted for c and $\frac{1}{2}b + 5$ is substituted for a.

We can actually also plug in here if we're careful. Starting with the first equation, pick values that work. For example, we might say that $a = 15$ and $b = 20$. The second equation then forces us to say that $c = 8$. From there, the third equation means that $d = 4$. Which answer choice will be true with those values? Only choice A will.

39. D
Parabolas

Because we know the properties of the equation of a parabola in standard form, we can answer this easily without a calculator just by looking at the graph. When a parabola's equation is in the form $y = ax^2 + bx + c$:

- The constant a tells us whether the parabola opens up or down (positive a opens up; negative a opens down).

- The constant c tells us the y-intercept.

- The x-coordinate of the vertex of the parabola will be $-\dfrac{b}{2a}$.

In this case, we see that the parabola opens down, so we want negative constant for the squared term, and we see the parabola has a positive y-intercept, so we want a positive constant term. Just knowing those two things eliminate all the wrong answers: choices A and B have negative y-intercepts, and choices B and C are parabolas that open up. That leaves D as the correct choice!

40. C
Exponents and Exponential Functions

Generally speaking, it's good to just know the basic exponential growth formula: $y = ab^x$, where a is a starting value and b is a growth (or decay) factor. In the case of percentage growth, as we have in this problem, that can be modified. Say r is the percentage growth, then the formula we'd use is $y = a(1 + r)^x$.

That's what we've got going on here. If population grows at 2% per year, then we know that the formula should have $(1 + 0.02)^x$ in it, which of course simplifies to 1.02^x. Just from that, we know the answer is choice C. The 10,000 in choice C also makes sense, because from the graph it looks like the population in 1981 in Town X was about 10,000.

One final note: when in doubt, test things out with a calculator. Pick a point on the graph that's easy to read (like about 12,000 in 1990, or about 14,000 in 1998) and see which answer choice lands close. 1990 and 1998 are 9 and 17 years from 1981, respectively. Look what choice C spits out:

$P(9) = 10{,}000 \times 1.02^9 \approx 11{,}951$

$P(17) = 10{,}000 \times 1.02^{17} \approx 14{,}002$

Pretty good, right? None of the other choices will get us as close.

41. 88
Translating between Words and Math; Binomial Squares and Difference of Two Squares

Translate the given statements into math:

$a > b$

$a + b = 11$

$a - b = 8$

Recognize that the thing we're asked about, $a^2 - b^2$, is a difference of two squares and can therefore be easily factored into $(a + b)(a - b)$. Conveniently, we have values for both of those factors!

$a^2 - b^2$

$= (a + b)(a - b)$

$= (11)(8)$

$= 88$

---

42. 2
Circles, Radians, and a Little More Trigonometry

For circle equation questions, we'll often be in the position of having to complete some squares. That's certainly the case here.

$x^2 + y^2 - 10x + 14y = -70$

$(x^2 - 10x) + (y^2 + 14y) = -70$

To complete those squares, we'll need to add 25 to the first term and 49 to the second term. Offsetting those, we'll have to add $25 + 49 = 74$ to the right side of the equation, taking us from –70 to 4.

$(x^2 - 10x + 25) + (y^2 + 14y + 49) = 4$

Factor:

$(x - 5)^2 + (y + 7)^2 = 4$

Now, remember that the standard circle equation is $(x - h)^2 + (y - k)^2 = r^2$, where the center of the circle is (h, k) and the radius is r.

Therefore, the circle in this question has a center at $(5, -7)$ and, more importantly, a radius of 2.

---

43. 5
Parabolas

The easiest way to go here might be to plug the point we know, $(0, 8)$ into the given equation and solve for a:

$y = -(x - a)^2 + 9$

$0 = -(8 - a)^2 + 9$

$0 = -(64 - 16a - a^2) + 9$

$0 = -64 + 16a - a^2 + 9$

$0 = -a^2 + 16a - 55$

$0 = a^2 - 16a + 55$

$0 = (a - 5)(a - 11)$

That tells us that $a = 5$ or $a = 11$. Since we want the least possible value, our answer is 5.

---

44. 3, 10
Parabolas

Remember: when given a point and a function, we're probably going to have to plug the point into the function.

$f(x) = x^2 - 13x + 35$

$5 = k^2 - 13k + 35$

$0 = k^2 - 13k + 30$

From there, we can factor!

$0 = (k - 3)(k - 10)$

Of course, that means the two acceptable values for k are 3 and 10.

---

45. B
Algebraic Manipulation; Ratios and Proportionality

The math on this one isn't that hard, but it's still pretty easy to get fooled! Let's start by plugging all the numbers we know into the equation and simplifying.

$$P = 5w + \frac{2}{3}t + \frac{3}{10}m$$

$$54 = 5(3) + \frac{2}{3}t + \frac{3}{10}(30)$$

$$54 = 15 + \frac{2}{3}t + 9$$

$$54 = 24 + \frac{2}{3}t$$

Now let's solve for t:

$$30 = \frac{2}{3}t$$

$$45 = t$$

Wait! Don't pick C! 45 is t, the number of minutes spent driving, but we need the driver's average speed in miles per hour! Don't lose important points by not being careful with units.

Average speed is calculated by dividing distance traveled by time spent traveling. Average Speed in miles per hour is:

$$\frac{\text{miles traveled}}{\text{hours spent traveling}}$$

We know the distance is 30 miles, and we know 45 minutes is $\frac{3}{4}$ of an hour. So we can calculate the average speed:

$$\text{Avg. Speed}_{\text{MPH}} = \frac{30 \text{ miles}}{\frac{3}{4} \text{ hours}}$$

$$\text{Avg. Speed}_{\text{MPH}} = 40 \text{ miles per hour}$$

---

46. D
Parabolas

The best way to get this one is to remember that when we get a parabola in factored form (like the one given), we know the parabola's zeros. In this case, the parabola will have zeros at $x = 5$ and $x = p$.

Because parabolas are symmetrical about their vertices, the x-coordinate of the vertex will always be the average of the x-coordinates of the parabola's zeros (or any other two points on the parabola with the same y-coordinate).

In other words, we know that 9 will be the average of 5 and p.

$$\frac{5 + p}{2} = 9$$

$$5 + p = 18$$

$$p = 13$$

---

47. B
Lines

The thing to remember about lines that pass through the origin is that we can tell their slope from any non-origin point. If a line passes through the point (a, b), we can calculate the slope using the standard formula:

$$\text{slope} = \frac{b-0}{a-0} = \frac{b}{a}$$

See how the zeros cancel out?

Therefore, for both points in an answer choice to be on the same line that passes through the origin, they both must indicate the same slope. Only choice B accomplishes that:

$$\frac{3}{\left(-\frac{1}{3}\right)} = -9$$

$$\frac{-1}{\left(\frac{1}{9}\right)} = -9$$

48. 0.5, 1/2
Exponents and Exponential Functions

This question involves exponents at a basic level, but it's really more of an algebraic manipulation question. To solve, clean up the left-hand side by adding up the numerator and then simplifying the fraction.

$$\frac{a^3 + a^3 + a^3}{6} = a^4$$

$$\frac{3a^3}{6} = a^4$$

$$\frac{a^3}{2} = a^4$$

$$\frac{1}{2}a^3 = a^4$$

Then divide and we're done!

$$\frac{1}{2} = \frac{a^4}{a^3}$$

$$\frac{1}{2} = a$$

49. C
Angles, Triangles, and Polygons

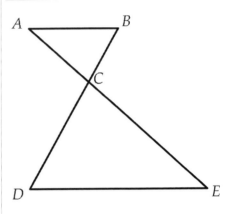

What we need to recognize right away in this question is that we're dealing with similar triangles. Angles ACB and ECD are vertical angles, so they're congruent. Because of the parallel segments $\overline{AB}$ and $\overline{DE}$, angles A and E are congruent and angles B and D are congruent. So, yeah. Similar triangles.

We're told that $AB = 5$ and $DE = 10$, so we know that the sides of the small triangle are half the length of the sides of the large triangle. Therefore, if $BC = \frac{10}{3}$, then the corresponding side in the larger triangle must be twice as long: $DC = \dfrac{20}{3}$.

To find the length of $\overline{BD}$, just add BC and DC.

$$\frac{10}{3} + \frac{20}{3} = \frac{30}{3} = 10$$

---

50. 17
Polynomials

Remember: when we have equivalent polynomials, their corresponding coefficients are equal. That means if $ax^2 + bx + c = px^2 + qx + r$, then $a = p$, $b = q$, and $c = r$. Cool? Cool.

To use that fact to solve this, first FOIL out the right-hand side.

$$3x^2 + bx + 24 = (3x + 8)(x + a)$$
$$3x^2 + bx + 24 = 3x^2 + 3ax + 8x + 8a$$

From there we know that the constants, with no x-terms, are equal. In other words, $24 = 8a$, which of course means $3 = a$.

Use that to solve for the value of b. The x-coefficient terms must also be equal: $bx = 3ax + 8x$. If $a = 3$, then $bx = 3(3)x + 8x = 17x$. That means $b = 17$.

---

51. A
Absolute Value

Remember that we can convert absolute value inequalities thusly: $|x - y| < z$ can be rewritten as $-z < x - y < z$.

Use that fact to convert answer choices until we get what we want:

the answer choice that can be manipulated to be equivalent to $198 \le m \le 212$.

Here's how that works with choice A, which happens to be the right answer:

$$|m - 205| \le 7$$
$$-7 \le m - 205 \le 7$$
$$198 \le m \le 212$$

A useful way to think about the initially-less-intuitive absolute value range is this: $|m - 205| \le 7$ is really just saying that m can't be farther than 7 away from 205. That makes sense! 205 is the middle of the range we care about, and 7 is the distance from 205 to 198 or 212.

---

52. 6
Measures of Central Tendency and Variability

The trick here is recognizing that the median of 39 data points will be the 20th point once the points are in order. (A shortcut to find the position of the median of an odd number of data points is $\dfrac{n+1}{2}$. In this case, $n = 39$ so the position is 20. Personally, I find it helpful to remember that in a list of 39 numbers, there will be 19 numbers smaller than the median and 19 numbers bigger than the median. That 20th number, counting from either end, is the median.)

Anyway, once we recognize that, all we need to do is count to 20!

Start from the right since the numbers are bigger there. There are 8 9's, 5 8's, and 6 7's. $8 + 5 + 6 = 19$,

146

so the next number, a 6, will be the 20th point from the top: the median!

We can also count from the left, and of course we'll get the same result. There are 5 1's, 2 2's, 4 3's, 1 4, and 3 5's. $5 + 2 + 4 + 1 + 3 = 15$. Now add the 6's: there are 5 of them, so the last 6 counting from the left will be the 20th number.

---

53. C
Functions

There are a few ways to think about this, but my approach is usually a "what has to happen?" one. In other words, what has to happen to $x + 7$ to turn it into $5x + 5$? Whatever it is that has to happen, that's what the function will do to anything that's put into it.

The first thing that needs to happen to $x + 7$ to turn it into $5x + 5$ is multiplication by 5. There's no way to turn x into $5x$ without doing that! However, multiplying by 5 alone gives us $5(x + 7) = 5x + 355$. We're not there yet.

The next thing we have to do is subtract! If we take away 30, then we'll be where we want to be: $(5x + 35) - 30 = 5x + 5$.

So, let's recap. We figured out that to turn $x + 7$ into $5x + 5$, we first need to multiply by 5, and then we need to subtract 30. Therefore, we can define the f function like so:

$$f(x) = 5x - 30$$

We can check our work here, of course, and we should! If $f(x) = 5x - 30$, then:

$$f(x + 7) = 5(x + 7) - 30$$
$$f(x + 7) = 5x + 35 - 30$$
$$f(x + 7) = 5x + 5$$

Nice.

Now that we know $f(x) = 5x - 30$, it's easy to calculate $f(2x)$:

$$f(2x) = 5(2x) - 30$$
$$f(2x) = 10x - 30$$

---

54. 6
Ratios and Proportionality

To solve this question, we need to convert between part:part ratios (like boys:girls) to part:whole ratios (like boys:students). The way I like to do this is to add the numbers in the original ratio to create a new ratio.

If there are 5 boys to 4 girls in Class A, then there are 5 boys for every $5 + 4 = 9$ total students. In other words, $\frac{5}{9}$ of the 27 students in Class A are boys, and $\frac{4}{9}$ are girls. $\frac{5}{9} \times 27 = 15$ And $\frac{4}{9} \times 27 = 12$, so there are 15 boys and 12 girls in Class A.

Class B is easy: if the ratio is 1 to 1, then half the class is boys and the other half is girls. There are 17 boys and 17 girls in Class B.

In Class C, $\frac{4}{11}$ of the students are boys and $\frac{7}{11}$ of the students are girls. $\frac{4}{11} \times 33 = 12$ And $\frac{7}{11} \times 33 = 21$, so there are 12 boys and 21 girls in Class C.

In total, then, there are $15 + 17 + 12 = 44$ boys and $12 + 17 + 21 = 50$ girls. Therefore, there are $50 - 44 = 6$ more girls than boys in those three classes.

---

55. 3
Exponents and Exponential Functions

Start by simplifying the numerator on the left. When we raise an exponential expression to another power, we multiply the exponents.

$$\frac{3^{x)^2}}{3^{3x}} = \frac{1}{27}$$

$$\frac{3^{2x}}{3^{3x}} = \frac{1}{27}$$

Now we're ready to simplify the fraction. When we divide two exponential expressions with the same base, we subtract the exponents.

$$3^{2x-3x} = \frac{1}{27}$$

$$3^{-x} = \frac{1}{27}$$

Finally, remember that a negative exponent is the same as the inverse of the positive exponent. In other words:

$$\frac{1}{3^x} = \frac{1}{27}$$

$$3^x = 27$$

$$x = 3$$

---

56. 5
Measures of Central Tendency and Variability

Here's the fast way to get the median out of a histogram. First, note that if the total number of participants in the contest was 81, there will be 40 participants who did the same or worse than the median, and 40 participants who did the same or better. Then there's the median participant, #41, right there in the middle.

Because we know the median score will be the 41st score in the list when the list is in order, all you need to do is start counting up from the left side or the right side until you get past 41. The bar that pushes you past 41, from either side, will contain the median. Here, I'll count from both sides.

Counting from the left we have $3 + 0 + 6 + 15 + 11 = 35$ people in the bars before 5 free throws made. Adding the 9 from the bar for 5 shots made gets us up to 44, past the 41st score, so the median is 5.

Counting from the right we have $1 + 7 + 3 + 11 + 15 = 37$ in the bars to the right of 5 free throws made. Adding the 9 from the bar for 5 shots made gets us up to 46, past the 41st score, so the median is 5.

57. D
Angles, Triangles, and Polygons

The sum of the interior angles in a polygon with n sides is equal to $(n-2)\,180$. If it's a regular polygon with equal sides and equal angles like the one in this question, then the measure of each interior angle can be calculated by dividing by n:

$$\frac{(n-2)\,180}{n}$$

Because the question gives the measure of the interior angles, all we need to do is solve:

$$162 = \frac{(n-2)\,180}{n}$$

$$162n = (n-2)\,180$$

$$162n = 180n - 360$$

$$-18n = -360$$

$$n = 20$$

So there are 20 sides in the polygon. Since each one has a length of 7 inches, the perimeter is $20 \times 7 = 140$ inches.

58. C
Angles, Triangles, and Polygons

Let's tackle this one in a few steps. First, use vertical and supplemental angle rules to fill in all the angles you can based on the measures you're given.

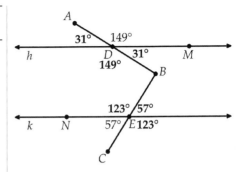

Now take either $\overline{AB}$ or $\overline{CB}$ (either one will do) and extend it to create a transversal. I'm going to extend $\overline{CB}$. Because we have parallel lines, we know all the angles we've filled in at point E will translate to the new intersection we create.

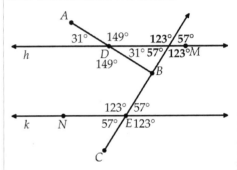

Now we have a triangle with angles measuring $31°$ and $57°$. Every triangle's angles add up to $180°$, so the third angle in that triangle must measure $180° - 57° - 31° = 92°$.

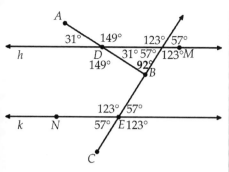

$\angle ABC$ is the supplement of that 92° angle (i.e., it makes a straight line with that angle) so its measure must be $180° - 92° = 88°$.

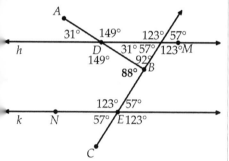

9. B
Exponents and Exponential Functions

To crack this one open, let's rewrite the left side of the equation thusly:

$$2^a + 2^a = 2^{b+3}$$

$$2\left(2^a\right) = 2^{b+3}$$

Now, noting that $2 = 2^1$, apply the exponent rule that says that when we multiply two exponential expressions with the same base, we add the exponents:

$$2^1 \times 2^a = 2^{b+3}$$

$$2^{a+1} = 2^{b+3}$$

From there, we can just say that:

$$a + 1 = b + 3$$

$$a - b = 3 - 1$$

$$a - b = 2$$

60. 12
Polynomials

The function will be undefined when its denominator equals zero. Given that we know the function is undefined when $x = 1$, we can substitute into the denominator and solve for a without much fuss:

$$0 = 1^2 - a(1) + 11$$

$$0 = 12 - a$$

$$a = 12$$

And...that's it! Wow, that was fast.

61. D
Solving Systems of Linear Equations; Lines

The first thing we'll want to do here is put both inequalities into slope-intercept form. Then, well, I'm feeling like graphing on this one. :)

$$2y + 3 > x - 2$$

$$2y > x - 5$$

$$y > \frac{1}{2}x - \frac{5}{2}$$

$$y - 8 < 2x - 5$$

$$y < 2x + 3$$

Now we can graph! I'll show shading in my figure because it looks awesome, but really we just need to see the lines and remember which inequality is greater than and which is less than.

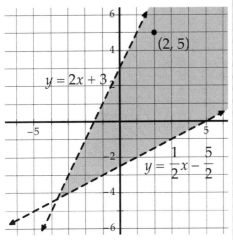

Cool, right? The shading represent the solution set, below the $y = 2x + 3$ line, and above the $y = \frac{1}{2}x - \frac{5}{2}$ line. All you need to do from there is check which points in the answer choices fall into that shaded region. The only one that does is $(2, 5)$.

If graphing's not exciting you, you can also get this one relatively quickly by backsolving. Just try each choice in *both* inequalities. The first one that satisfies both is the right answer. Here's what that looks like with choice D:

$2(5) + 3 > (2) - 2$

$13 > 0$

$(3) - 8 < 2(2) - 5$

$-3 < -1$

Since both of those inequalities work out true, choice D is in the solution set of the system of inequalities.

---

62. 44
Measures of Central Tendency and Variability

Many average questions like this one are really questions about sums, and this one definitely is. Start by figuring out the sum of the ages in the room when all 19 people are in there. If the average age is 8, then the sum of the ages will be $8 \times 19 = 152$.

Now figure out the sum of the ages once the one adult we care about leaves. The new average in the room becomes 6, and there are now 18 people in the room, so the new sum is $6 \times 18 = 108$.

How old must the person who left be if the sum of the ages in the room went from 152 to 108? $152 - 108 = 44$.

---

63. 22
Functions

The fastest way to solve this one is to set $x + 3 = 10$ and solve. If $x + 3 = 10$ then $x = 7$, so:

$f(10)$

$= f(7 + 3)$

$= 3(7) + 1$

$= 22$

We can also take a few extra steps and figure out a general form for $f(x)$ given the general form for $f(x + 3)$, which is a good skill to practice even if it's not 100% needed on this question. The way I usually approach this is to remember that functions act kinda like a car wash—they do the same thing to every input they get. So if we know what the function does to $x + 3$, we should be able to figure out what it'll do to x.

$f(x + 3) = 3x + 1$. That means, first and foremost, that there's a multiplication by 3 that happens in the function. However, just multiplying $3(x + 3)$ would give us $3x + 9$, so there must also be subtraction of 8 to get down to $3x + 1$. In other words, the f function multiplies its input by 3, and then subtracts 8 from that result. $f(x) = 3x - 8$.

To ensure we're right, evaluate that for $f(x + 3)$ and make sure we land on $3x + 1$:

$f(x) = 3x - 8$

$f(x + 3) = 3(x + 3) - 8$

$f(x + 3) = 3x + 9 - 8$

$f(x + 3) = 3x + 1$

Yep, looks good! Now just evaluate $f(10)$:

$f(x) = 3x - 8$

$f(10) = 3(10) - 8$

$f(10) = 30 - 8$

$f(10) = 22$

---

4. C
Plugging in; Polynomials

If you get a question like this, where your job is to figure out equivalent expressions, and those expressions only have one variable...PLUG IN! This is a huge opportunity to get a question right that many of your fellow students

will miss, and do it without much math!

The only math I want to do first is factor out a 2, since that'll make plugging in even easier.

$$\frac{8x + 4}{2x + 8} = \frac{4x + 2}{x + 4}$$

There, that's better. Now, let's pick a value for x. I'm a fan of using small numbers—let's try $x = 2$. If $x = 2$, then $\dfrac{4x + 2}{x + 4} = \dfrac{4(2) + 2}{2 + 4} = \dfrac{10}{6}$.

Which answer choice *also* equals $\dfrac{10}{6}$ when $x = 2$?

Because we picked an easy number like 2 to work with, we can check choices very quickly.

A) $x + \dfrac{2}{x} = 2 + \dfrac{2}{2} = 3$ ← NOPE.

B) $4x + \dfrac{1}{2} = 4(2) + \dfrac{1}{2} = 8.5$ ← NOPE.

C) $4 - \dfrac{14}{x + 4} = 4 - \dfrac{14}{2 + 4} = 4 - \dfrac{14}{6}$
$= \dfrac{24}{6} - \dfrac{14}{6} = \dfrac{10}{6}$ ← YAAS!

D) $4 + \dfrac{7}{x + 4} = 4 + \dfrac{7}{2 + 4} = 4 + \dfrac{7}{6}$
$= \dfrac{24}{6} + \dfrac{7}{6} = \dfrac{31}{6}$ ← NOPE.

It's really important to remember that, when plugging in, we must check every choice even after we find one that works, just to make sure we haven't inadvertently picked a number to plug in that would make more than one choice work.

Wait, what? You want to do polynomial division instead???

$$2x + 8 \overline{\smash{\big)}\ 8x + 4}$$

$$\begin{array}{r} 4 \\ 2x + 8 \overline{\smash{\big)}\ 8x + 4} \\ \underline{-(8x + 32)} \\ -28 \end{array}$$

That means there's a remainder of –28 with a divisor of $2x + 8$. That's the same as saying:

$$\frac{8x + 4}{2x + 8} = 4 - \frac{14}{2x + 8}$$

$$\frac{8x + 4}{2x + 8} = 4 - \frac{14}{x + 4}$$

65. 9
Solving Systems of Linear Equations

Remember that a system of linear equations will only have an infinite number of solutions when both equations represent the exact same line—they must have the same slope and the same y-intercept. So our first step here should be to put both equations into slope-intercept form.

$$3x - \frac{1}{3}y = a$$

$$-\frac{1}{3}y = -3x + a$$

$$y = 9x - 3a$$

$$ax - y = 27$$

$$-y = -ax + 27$$

$$y = ax - 27$$

From there, we might already see the answer, but if not we can set

the slopes and y-intercepts equal to each other.

Setting the slopes equal to each other simply gives us $9 = a$, which is pretty great. Setting the y-intercepts equal gives you $-3a = -27$, which of course also simplifies to $9 = a$.

66. 9.75, 39/4
Solving Systems of Linear Equations

Solve this one by elimination. Multiply the first equation by 2 to cancel out the y-terms:

$$6x + 2y = 22$$
$$10x - 2y = 2$$

Now add the equations together. The y-terms cancel out and we're left with something that's easy to solve for x: $16x = 24$.

Of course, that means $x = \frac{24}{16} = \frac{3}{2}$.

Now just solve for y. Pick either equation.

$$10\left(\frac{3}{2}\right) - 2y = 2$$

$$\frac{30}{2} - 2y = 2$$

$$15 - 2y = 2$$

$$-2y = -13$$

$$y = \frac{13}{2}$$

Now that we have values for x and y, multiply to get the answer we seek.

$$xy = \left(\frac{3}{2}\right)\left(\frac{13}{2}\right) = \frac{39}{4}$$

67. .285, .286, 2/7
Quadratics

The domain of the function will exclude the zeros of the polynomial in the denominator—we needn't pay any attention at all to the numerator to solve this question. Just solve $0 = 7x^2 - 2x - 5$.

Since the polynomial isn't easy to factor, let's throw it into the quadratic formula.

$$x = \frac{-(-2) \pm \sqrt{(-2)^2 - 4(7)(-5)}}{2(7)}$$

$$x = \frac{2 \pm \sqrt{144}}{14}$$

$$x = \frac{2 \pm 12}{14}$$

$$x = \frac{1}{7} \pm \frac{6}{7}$$

In other words, the values of a and b are 1 and $-\frac{5}{7}$. Since we're asked for the value of $a + b$, the correct answer is $1 + \left(-\frac{5}{7}\right) = \frac{2}{7}$.

68. 9
Parabolas; Quadratics

It's a good idea to know the basic shape of parabolas and their standard forms so that we can do questions like this easily without a calculator.

This parabola is given in vertex form—from looking at the equation we see that it opens downwards from a vertex of $(7, 4)$. The normal shape of a parabola with a leading coefficient of 1 or –1 tells us that it

will travel 2 units left or right as it travels 4 units down to the x-axis. 2 units to the right of $x = 7$ will put you at the greater of the two x-intercepts at $x = 9$.

If you're not comfortable with that kind of analysis, you can still solve this question without a calculator: you just need to FOIL, simplify, and then factor.

$$y = -(x - 7)^2 + 4$$

$$y = -(x^2 - 14x + 49) + 4$$

$$y = -x^2 + 14x - 49 + 4$$

$$y = -x^2 + 14x - 45$$

$$y = -(x^2 - 14x + 45)$$

$$y = -(x - 5)(x - 9)$$

From that, you can see that the parabola will have zeros at 5 and 9, so again you see that the greater of the x-intercepts of the parabola is 9.

69. 35
Data Analysis 1; Measures of Central Tendency and Variability

The first step to solving this is calculating the Team 1's score. Cross out the highest and lowest scores (63 and 33, respectively) and then find the average of the remaining three scores.

$$\text{Score}_{T1} = \frac{44 + 34 + 50}{3} = 42.\overline{6}$$

To deal with Team 2, first eliminate the highest score, 66.

Now let's calculate Team 2's score if Player 10's ended up being the lowest and thus inconsequential. Can Team 2 win without Player 10?

$$\text{Score}_{\text{T2 without P10}} = \frac{47 + 47 + 31}{3} = 41.\overline{6}$$

Nope, Team 2 can't win without Player 10's score! That means Player 9's score will have to end up being the lowest on Team 2. Player 10's score must be combined with two 47 scores to beat Team 1. So let's call Player 10's score x and solve.

$$\frac{44 + 34 + 50}{3} < \frac{47 + 47 + x}{3}$$

$$44 + 34 + 50 < 47 + 47 + x$$

$$128 < 94 + x$$

$$34 < x$$

Since x must be an integer, the lowest it can be is 35.

---

70. A
Backsolving; Quadratics

Before we get into the algebra here, I want to point out that this is an excellent backsolve question. There are only a few possible numbers in the answer choices, and substituting them into the given equation won't take long at all. Plus, even if we do this question the math way, we'll end up having to substitute back into the original equation, so backsolve should really be looked at as a major time saver here. Hold that thought.

The math: start by squaring the equation. That'll give us a quadratic we can set equal to 0 and solve.

$$(5 - x)^2 = \left(\sqrt{x - 3}\right)^2$$

$$25 - 10x + x^2 = x - 3$$

$$28 - 11x + x^2 = 0$$

$$x^2 - 11x + 28 = 0$$

$$(x - 7)(x - 4) = 0$$

So, there we have it: $x = 4$ or $x = 7$, right? WRONG! Remember, we squared this equation in the beginning to get rid of a square root. When we do that, we need to check for extraneous solutions! So put both 4 and 7 back into the original equation to see what happens.

$$5 - x = \sqrt{x - 3}$$

$$5 - 4 = \sqrt{4 - 3}$$

$$1 = \sqrt{1}$$

$$1 = 1 \leftarrow \text{That works!}$$

$$5 - 7 = \sqrt{7 - 3}$$

$$-2 = \sqrt{4}$$

$$-2 \neq 2 \leftarrow \text{That } \textit{doesn't} \text{ work!}$$

As you can see, setting $x = 4$ gives you a true equation, but setting $x = 7$ does not. The solution set therefore contains only 4.

Now, back to what I was saying at the beginning of this solution about backsolving. Pardon my caps: WE HAD TO TRY 4 AND 7 *EVEN AFTER* WE DID THE MATH. WE COULD HAVE SAVED A LOT OF TIME BY JUST TRYING 4 AND 7 AT THE START. AS SOON AS WE SAW THAT 4 WORKED AND 7 DIDN'T, WE'D HAVE ELIMINATED EVERY CHOICE BUT THE CORRECT ONE RIGHT AWAY!

71. C
Circles, Radians, and a Little More Trigonometry

The standard form for a circle equation is $(x-h)^2 + (y-k)^2 = r^2$, where (h,k) is the center of the circle and r is the radius. Before we can determine the radius of this circle, we need to complete two squares to get into standard form.

$$x^2 + y^2 + 10x + 2y = 64$$

$$x^2 + 10x + y^2 + 2y = 64$$

To complete those squares, we'll need to add 25 to the first one, and 1 to the second one. Therefore, we'll have to add 25 + 1 = 26 to the right side to keep the equation balanced.

$$x^2 + 10x + 25 + y^2 + 2y + 1 = 64 + 26$$

$$(x+5)^2 + (y+1)^2 = 90$$

From that, we see that the value of r^2 in the standard equation is 90. Take the square root to find r.

$$r^2 = 90$$

$$r = \sqrt{90}$$

$$r = (\sqrt{9})(\sqrt{10})$$

$$r = 3\sqrt{10}$$

72. C
Data Analysis 2; Lines

Note that all the answers are in slope-intercept form. The thing to zero in on is that the big difference between the answer choices is slope—the possible intercepts are all plausible enough given the picture.

Pick two points (they don't actually have to be points on the scatterplot!) that feel like they should be on or near the line of best fit, and figure out the slope between them. Looks to me like it makes sense to use $(8, 60)$ and $(16, 110)$.

The slope between those two points is $\dfrac{110-60}{16-8} = 6.25$.

The only answer choice with a slope even close to that is choice C.

73. 4
Polynomials

When two polynomials are equivalent, then all their corresponding coefficients are equal. In this case, the coefficients of x^2 are equal, the coefficients of x are equal, and the constant terms are equal.

FOIL out the left hand side to see where we stand:

$$(2x - a)^2 = 4x^2 - bx + a + 12$$

$$4x^2 - 4ax + a^2 = 4x^2 - ba + a + 12$$

Obviously the $4x^2$ terms are equal. We also know that $-4ax = -bx$ and, most importantly, that $a^2 = a + 12$. Since that last equation has only a's in it and that's what we're looking for, solve it!

$$a^2 = a + 12$$

$$a^2 - a - 12 = 0$$

$$(a + 3)(a - 4) = 0$$

So $a = -3$ or $a = 4$. Because the question says that a is positive, we know the answer must be 4.

74. C
Percents and Percent Change

The first thing we need to do here is figure out how many people are on this task force to start with. We know that $30\% + 15\% + 40\% = 85\%$ of the task force is sales, marketing, or product design, so that means the 3 executives must comprise 15% of the task force. 3 is 15% of what?

$$3 = \frac{15}{100}x$$

$$20 = x$$

Now, let's figure out how many product designers we're starting with. What is 40% of 20?

$$\frac{40}{100} \times 20 = 8$$

If we're starting with 8 product designers and we add 2 more, we'll have 10. But be careful! We're also increasing the total size of the task force from 20 to 22! So the question we're asking is: 10 is what percent of 22?

$$10 = \frac{y}{100} \times 22$$

$$\frac{1,000}{22} = y$$

$$45.\overline{45} = y$$

There it is. If the task force were expanded to include 2 more product designers, product

designers would make up about 45% of the task force.

75. 16
Polynomials

The key to solving this one is remembering that the corresponding coefficients of equivalent polynomials are equal. That's a mouthful, but what it means is that if the equation is true for all values of x, then the coefficient of x^2 on the left will equal the coefficient of x^2 on the right, the coefficient of x on the left will equal the coefficient of x on the right, and the constant term on the left will equal the constant term on the right.

Let's get started by doing all the multiplication we can:

$$(x + a)(2x - b) = ax^2 + (2a - b)x - 32$$

$$2x^2 - bx + 2ax - ab = ax^2 + 2ax - bx - 3$$

What we know from there, right away without even messing with the x-terms, is that $2 = a$ (those are the x^2 coefficients) and $-ab = -32$ (those are the constants).

Substituting for a, we find that $-2b = -32$ and therefore $b = 16$.

76. C
Circles, Radians, and a Little More Trigonometry; Angles, Triangles, and Polygons

Recognize that $\overline{AB}$ is a radius of both circles, so each circle has a radius of 8 inches and therefore a circumference of 16π inches. From there, note that drawing in a couple more radii, like so, creates equilateral triangles:

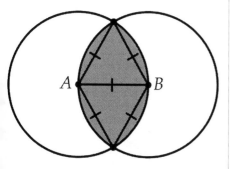

All the angles in an equilateral triangle measure 60°, so the central angles that correspond to the arcs that make up the shaded region measure 120°.

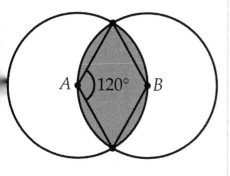

120° is $\frac{1}{3}$ of 360°, so each of the two arcs is $\frac{1}{3}$ of the full circumference of 16π.

$$\frac{16\pi}{3} + \frac{16\pi}{3} = \frac{32\pi}{3}$$

---

7. D
Absolute Value

Without a calculator to help graph this, we'll need to either use finely honed knowledge of how graph translations and reflections work

with $y = |x|$ (which makes a V-shape at the origin) or do a little trial and error to see which choices won't produce any negative y-values when $x > 0$. This works, of course, because $y < 0$ and $x > 0$ in Quadrant IV.

I encourage you to play with these answer choices in your calculator after the fact because I think that can help you develop the sense to be able to solve this without plugging in values, but for simplicity's sake I'm just going to make a chart showing y-values here for $x = 1$ through $x = 3$. This is how I'd do this problem on test day to make sure I wasn't making any silly mistakes.

	x equals		
	1	2	3
A) $\lvert 3-x\rvert -1$	1	0	−1
B) $\lvert x-1\rvert -3$	−3	−2	−1
C) $1-\lvert 3-x\rvert$	−1	0	1
D) $\lvert 3+x\rvert -1$	3	4	5

As you can see, we don't need to try many positive values of x before we can eliminate all the wrong answer choices. Only choice D remains after trying only 3 values of x!

---

78. 13
Solving Systems of Linear Equations

Let's get this one by elimination. To do that, multiply the first equation by the lowest common denominator: 20.

$$20\left(\frac{1}{5}x + \frac{3}{4}y\right) = (3)20$$

$$4x + 15y = 60$$

Now we can eliminate the y terms simply by adding the equations, and solve for x:

$$4x + 15y = 60$$
$$\underline{+\ x - 15y = 5}$$
$$5x + 0y = 65$$

$$5x = 65$$

$$x = 13$$

---

79. 80
Circles, Radians, and a Little More Trigonometry

Remember: circle parts are proportional. An arc lengh will be the same proportion of the circumference as the angle of the arc is of 360°:

$$\frac{\text{central angle measure}}{360°} = \frac{\text{arc length}}{C}$$

We know an arc length, and we know a radius. From the radius, we can calculate a circumference, and then all we need to do is solve for the central angle. So let's go!

Circumference is $2\pi r$, so in this case it's $2\pi(45) = 90\pi$.

We'll use that to find the proportion of the given arc length to the whole circumference, and then solve for the central angle's measure:

$$\frac{\text{central angle measure}}{360°} = \frac{20\pi}{90\pi}$$

$$\frac{\text{central angle measure}}{360°} = \frac{2}{9}$$

$$\text{central angle measure} = \frac{2}{9} \times 360°$$

$$\text{central angle measure} = 80°$$

---

80. D
Circles, Radians, and a Little More Trigonometry

Get this one the fast way by drawing the circle. We know the standard form of a circle with radius r and center (h, k) is $(x - h)^2 + (y - k)^2 = r^2$. Therefore, we know that the equation you're given is a circle centered at $(3, -4)$ with radius 3. So draw that.

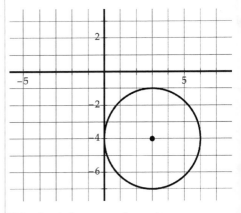

We don't have to draw it very accurately at all to be able to eliminate choices A and C. We should also note that choice B would be in completely the wrong quadrant. Therefore, without having to do much math, we can conclude that since choices A, B, and C are not correct, choice D must be correct!

If that's not good enough for you and you just need to see the math, make a 30°-60°-90° triangle. The radius of 3 must be the hypotenuse, so the short leg will be $\frac{3}{2}$ and the long leg will be $\frac{3\sqrt{3}}{2}$. If you start at the center of $(3, -4)$, go left $\frac{3}{2}$ units, then go up $\frac{3\sqrt{3}}{2}$ units, you land on the point in choice D.

---

81. 9
Angles, Triangles, and Polygons

The best way to get this one is to draw the given points:

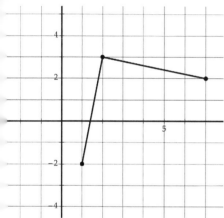

This isn't very mathematical, but count the up-and-over steps from the first point to the second, and from the second to the third. You'll see that the first side goes up 5 and right 1, and the second side goes right 5 and down 1. To figure out where the fourth vertex is, simply follow the same pattern: either move down 5 and left 1 from the

third point or go right 5 and down 1 from the first. Like so:

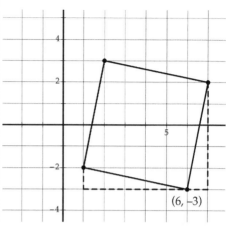

So the final point $(a, b) = (6, -3)$, which means $a = 6$ and $b = -3$. Therefore, $a - b = 6 - (-3) = 9$.

---

82. B
Solving Systems of Linear Equations; Lines

If a system of equations has no solutions, that means the graphs of those equations will never intersect. In the case of a system of *linear* equations, the only way that happens is if the two lines are parallel.

Parallel lines have the same slope, and the first line is given to you already in slope-intercept form—its slope is 3. Therefore, we need to find the value of $\frac{b}{a}$ that will result in the first equation also having a slope of 3. So let's put it into slope-intercept form:

$$ax - by = 11$$

$$-by = -ax + 11$$

$$y = \frac{a}{b}x - \frac{11}{b}$$

That tells us that the first line has a slope of $\frac{a}{b}$, which must equal 3 if the lines are to be parallel.

But wait, this question is sneaky! It asks for the reciprocal, $\frac{b}{a}$!

If $\frac{a}{b} = 3$, then $\frac{b}{a} = \frac{1}{3}$.

---

83. B
Functions

Think about this one in two steps. First, remember that the graph of $-f(x)$ will be the reflection of the graph of $f(x)$ about the x-axis. Like so:

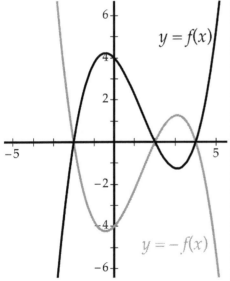

Now remember that multiplying by 2 outside the function will make all y-values twice as big. That won't change the x-intercepts, but it will make every other point on the

graph twice as far away from the x-axis.

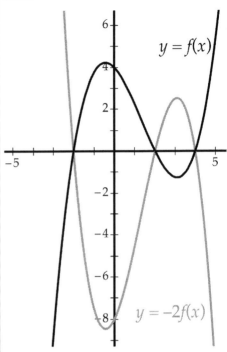

Since $(0, 4)$ is on the graph of $y = f(x)$, $(0, -8)$ is on the graph of $y = -2f(x)$, you can cross off choice A.

The x-intercepts of the graph don't change, so you can eliminate choices C and D: $(2, 0)$ and $(4, 0)$ will be on both $y = f(x)$ and $y = -2f(x)$.

That leaves only choice B. $(-4, 0)$ is on neither curve, so that's our answer.

---

84. B
Parabolas

Since this is a calculator allowed question, the fastest way to go might just be to graph each parabola. For a parabola to intersect a horizontal line like $y = 8$

exactly once, its vertex must be on that horizontal line. Just graph each equation and look for the one with its vertex at $y = 8$.

If you don't want to or can't do that, the other way to go is to manipulate each choice until you find one with its vertex at $y = 8$.

Look at choice B:

$$y = -\frac{1}{8}(x - 8)(x + 8)$$

$$y = -\frac{1}{8}(x^2 - 64)$$

$$y = -\frac{1}{8}x^2 + 8$$

That works! It's a parabola that opens down with its vertex (and y-intercept) at $y = 8$. None of the other choices will give you a vertex in the right place.

85. 2
Parabolas

There are a couple ways to go here, but to my mind the easiest way is to remember that a parabola is symmetrical about its vertex.

Since this parabola is in factored form, you know its zeros are at –6 and a. The vertex is on the $x = -2$ line, which means the root you know, $x = -6$, is a distance of 4 away. That means the other root, a must also be a distance of 4 from the $x = -2$ line. Count 4 steps to the right and you land on $x = 2$, so $a = 2$.

Of course, we can also substitute and solve algebraically.

$$-48 = 3(-2 - a)(-2 + 6)$$

$$-48 = 3(-2 - a)(4)$$

$$-48 = 12(-2 - a)$$

$$-4 = -2 - a$$

$$2 = a$$

86. 55
Translating between Words and Math

To solve this, first calculate how much money Marcy makes by working 48 hours. For the first 40 hours, she makes her normal rate of \$18 per hour. For the next 8 hours, she makes 150% of her normal rate (A.K.A. time-and-a-half). Marcy makes:

$$40(18) + 8\left(\frac{18 \times 150}{100}\right) = 936$$

If Louis makes \$64 more than Marcy, then he makes \$1,000. You know that he must work more than 40 hours to make that much (he makes less than Marcy does per hour and she had to work more than 40 hours to make \$936). If x is the number of hours Louis worked beyond 40:

$$40(16) + x\left(\frac{16 \times 150}{100}\right) = 1,000$$

$$640 + 24x = 1,000$$

$$24x = 360$$

$$x = 15$$

Be careful! The answer isn't 15! That's how many hours Louis worked beyond 40 hours. The total number of hours he worked includes the first 40, so the answer you want is $40 + 15 = 55$ hours.

87. 3.5, 7/2
Lines

The slopes of perpendicular lines are negative reciprocals, so the first thing we'll want to do is (as usual for line questions) put both equations into $y = mx + b$ form:

$4x + 7y = 30$

$7y = -4x + 30$

$y = -\dfrac{4}{7}x + \dfrac{30}{7}$

$ax - 2y = 5$

$2y = -ax + 5$

$y = \dfrac{a}{2}x - \dfrac{5}{2}$

The slope of the first line is $-\dfrac{4}{7}$, so the slope of the second line must be $\dfrac{7}{4}$ for the lines to be perpendicular. That means $\dfrac{a}{2} = \dfrac{7}{4}$, which means $a = \dfrac{7}{2}$.

88. C
Right Triangles and Basic Trigonometry

Before we do anything else, let's draw this so that we can keep points and sides straight.

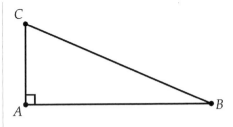

Because we know that $\sin B = \dfrac{5}{13}$, we know that $\dfrac{AC}{BC} = \dfrac{5}{13}$. That's a big clue if we remember our Pythagorean triples! We're dealing with a 5-12-13 triangle. Only not quite, because $5 + 12 + 13 \neq 150$. So we have to do a little algebra.

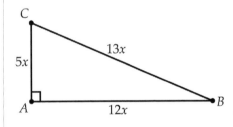

$5x + 12x + 13x = 150$

$30x = 150$

$x = 5$

If $x = 5$, and $AB = 12x$, then $AB = 60$.

89. B
Measures of Central Tendency and Variability

A box plot shows 5 data points to summarize a set of data: the minimum, the first quartile, the median, the third quartile, and the maximum. The whiskers reach out to the minimum and maximum; the box reaches out to the first and third quartiles.

Reading the minimum and maximum from the frequency graph is easy: 1 and 9.

Reading the median is a little trickier. The median of 39 data points will be the 20th point once the points are in order. (A shortcut to find the position of the median of an odd number of data points is $\frac{n+1}{2}$. In this case, $n = 39$ so the position is 20. Personally, I find it helpful to remember that in a list of 39 numbers, there will be 19 numbers smaller than the median and 19 numbers bigger than the median. That 20th number, counting from either end, is the median.)

Anyway, once we recognize that, all we need to do is count to 20! Start from either side and count to 20. From the left, there are 5 1's, 2 2's, 4 3's, 1 4, and 3 5's. 5 + 2 + 4 + 1 + 3 = 15. Now add the 6's: there are 5 of them, so the last 6 counting from the left will be the 20th number. That means the median is 6.

Now finally, the first and third quartiles. These are basically the medians of the subsets of data above and below the median. So the first quartile is the median of the first 19 numbers in the set, and the third quartile is the median of the last 19 numbers in the set.

As we just did for the main median, we can do $\frac{19+1}{2} = 10$ and find the 10th number in the first half for the first quartile. There are

5 1's, 2 2's, and 4 3's, so one of the 3's is the 10th number. That means the first quartile is 3.

For the third quartile, we can find the 10th number from the right. There are 8 9's and 5 8's, which means the 10th number from the top is one of those 8's. Therefore, the third quartile is 8.

To summarize:

Minimum: 1
First Quartile: 3
Median: 6
Third Quartile: 8
Maximum: 9

Which box plot captures all the points? Choice B it is!

---

90. B
Measures of Central Tendency and Variability

We don't need to know much about standard deviation for the SAT (it appears only twice in released practice tests 1–8), but we should know that the standard deviation is a measure of the variability of a data set. The more the data is spread out away from the mean, the larger its standard deviation. The more concentrated the data is around its mean, the smaller its standard deviation.

In this case, 9 more scores of 5 (or any more scores of 5) would decrease the standard deviation because 5 is *very* close to the mean. (The actual mean, not that you need to calculate it, is 5.06.) The more 5s you add, the more the data in this set is concentrated near the mean, and the smaller the standard deviation becomes.

---

91. 12
Ratios and Proportionality

An algebraic solution to this one is probably most expedient. Using r for red fish and b for blue fish before any were sold, we can write the following equations from the given ratios:

$$\frac{r}{b} = \frac{4}{7}$$

$$\frac{r}{b-5} = \frac{3}{4}$$

Even though we want r, I can't resist the urge to solve for b first using substitution. Solve both equations for r:

$$r = \frac{4}{7}b$$

$$r = \frac{3}{4}(b-5)$$

Now set them equal:

$$\frac{4}{7}b = \frac{3}{4}(b-5)$$

And solve for b! Multiplying by 28 will clean those fractions right up.

$$28 \times \left(\frac{4}{7}b\right) = \left(\frac{3}{4}(b-5)\right) \times 28$$

$$16b = 21(b-5)$$

$$16b = 21b - 105$$

$$-5b = -105$$

$$b = 21$$

Remember, though: we're really looking for r, not b!

If $b = 21$, then we can use either of the original ratios to solve for r.

$$\frac{r}{b} = \frac{4}{7}$$

$$\frac{r}{21} = \frac{4}{7}$$

$$r = 21\left(\frac{4}{7}\right)$$

$$r = 12$$

---

92. 144
Right Triangles and Basic Trigonometry

In solving this one, it's really helpful to remember the 5-12-13 Pythagorean triple. The question tells us that we have a right triangle (the measure of $\angle B = 90°$) and that two of its sides are in a 5 to 13 ratio. That's enough for us to know that all three sides will be in a 5:12:13 ratio!

From there, we must remember what $\cos(\angle A)$ means. Cosine is the ratio of the lengths of the angle's adjacent leg to the hypotenuse (remember: SOH-CAH-TOA!) so $\cos(\angle A) = \frac{5}{13}$ means the leg next to $\angle A$ is the short one.

We can draw this now, right?

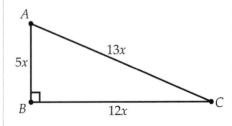

If $AB = 5x = 60$, then $x = 12$. That means $BC = 12x = 12(12) = 144$.

---

93. 144
Angles, Triangles, and Polygons

Generally speaking, the way to get a question like this is to just start solving for the angles we can solve for until eventually we can solve for the one we want. Try not to worry if you're not going the fastest possible way, just keep making progress.

If the measure of angle CAD is 26° and angle ACE is a right angle with a measure of 90°, then we can solve for the measure of angle CDA. Each triangle's angles add up 180°, so the last angle in triangle CAD must measure:

$180° - 90° - 26° = 64°$

Because angle ADE is supplementary, you know it must therefore measure:

$180° - 64° = 116°$

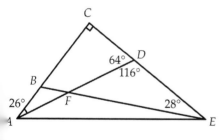

Now we're almost home. Because we know the measures of angles CDE and BEC, we can solve for the measure of angle DFE:

$180° - 116° - 28° = 36°$

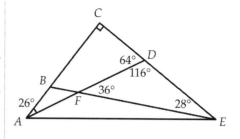

The angle we want, angle BFD, is supplementary to angle DFE, so we just need to subtract from 180° again:

$180° - 36° = 144°$

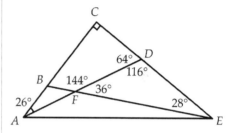

---

94. A
Lines

If you ask me, it's faster to test the answer choices here than to derive the right one. There are two things we must test the answer choices for: whether they go through $(2, 5)$ and whether they're parallel to $3x - 4y = 12$. Since all we need to do to test whether they pass through the point is plug the point into each equation and see if the equality holds, do that first and see if it eliminates any answers.

A) $-6(2) + 8(5) = 28 \leftarrow$ True!

B) $3(2) - 4(5) = -12 \leftarrow$ Not true.

C) $-3(2) + 4(5) = -14 \leftarrow$ Not true.

D) $-6(2)-8(5)=-52 \leftarrow$ True!

Now that we're down to only A and D, see which one is parallel to the given line. To do that, put each into slope-intercept form. First, the given line:

$3x - 4y = 12$

$-4y = -3x + 12$

$y = \dfrac{3}{4}x - 3$

Now put choice A in slope-intercept:

$-6x + 8y = 28$

$8y = 6x + 28$

$y = \dfrac{6}{8}x + \dfrac{28}{8}$

$y = \dfrac{3}{4}x + \dfrac{7}{2}$

Yep, that's the $\dfrac{3}{4}$ slope we're looking for! Choice A works! Now that we've shown that choice A has the right slope to be parallel to the given line *and* that choice A goes through $(2, 5)$, we're done!

---

95. 1080
Polynomials

This is a corresponding coefficients question, so get right to work FOILing to get both sides of the equation into standard form.

$ax^2 + 3x - b = (2x + 5)(3x - c)$

$ax^2 + 3x - b = 6x^2 - 2cx + 15x - 5c$

$ax^2 + 3x - b = 6x^2 + (15 - 2c)x - 5c$

From that we know three things:

- $a = 6$
- $3 = 15 - 2c$
- $-b = -5c$

Solve the second equation for c to get $c = 6$. Once we know $c = 6$ we know $-b = -5(6)$, which means $b = 30$.

The question asks for the value of abc, which is $6 \times 30 \times 6 = 1080$.

---

96. 78
Lines

First, let's figure out the equation of line n. We can do this because we know it's perpendicular to line m, which means its slope must be $\dfrac{1}{5}$, and we know it goes through the origin, which means its y-intercept is zero. Therefore, the equation of line n in slope-intercept form is $y = \dfrac{1}{5}x$.

From there, we can solve for b by plugging the intersection point into the equation above:

$b = \dfrac{1}{5}(15)$

$b = 3$

Once we have the value of b, it's smooth sailing to solve for a. Since we know the intersection point $(15, 3)$ is on line m, we can plug that use that point to solve for a:

$y = -5x + a$

$3 = -5(15) + a$

$3 = -75 + a$

$78 = a$

97. 12
Angles, Triangles, and Polygons

The easiest way to get this one is to recognize that the figure is a square with one quarter of it missing:

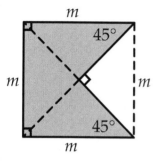

From there, we just need to do a little algebra. We know that the are of the square is m^2. We also know that $\frac{3}{4}$ of the area of the square (the shaded part above) is 108!

$$\frac{3}{4}m^2 = 108$$

$$m^2 = 144$$

$$m = 12$$

---

98. B
Circles, Radians, and a Little More Trigonometry

The key here is that if $\sin A = \cos B$, then A and B will be complementary angles (i.e., their sum will be 90° or $\frac{\pi}{2}$ radians). With that knowledge, all we need to do is see which choice gives us a sum of $\frac{\pi}{2}$ when the angle measures are added.

Choice A doesn't work:

$\frac{\pi}{8} + \frac{\pi}{8} = \frac{\pi}{4}$. That's not $\frac{\pi}{2}$, so move on.

Choice B *does* work:

$$\frac{\pi}{8} + \frac{\pi}{\left(\frac{8}{3}\right)} = \frac{\pi}{8} + \frac{3\pi}{8} = \frac{\pi}{2}\ \text{Wahoo!}$$

---

99. D
Lines; Solving Systems of Linear Equations

The first trick here is remembering that when lines are perpendicular, then their slopes are negative reciprocals. Because we know the slope of the first line is 3, we know the slope of the second line must be $-\frac{1}{3}$, so that's the value of a. We can solve from there.

The first equation simplifies:

$$y = 3x + 3a$$

$$y = 3x + 3\left(-\frac{1}{3}\right)$$

$$y = 3x - 1$$

The second equation just needs a little substitutin':

$$y = ax + 9$$

$$y = -\frac{1}{3}x + 9$$

From here we can solve however we like. I'll use the fact that both equations are already in $y =$ form to solve for x first:

$$3x - 1 = -\frac{1}{3}x + 9$$

$$\frac{10}{3}x = 10$$

$$10x = 30$$

$$x = 3$$

Great, now substitute to find y:

$$y = 3(3) - 1$$

$$y = 8$$

There we go—the intersection we seek is $(3, 8)$!

---

100. B
Polynomials; Quadratics

Pro-tip: we don't need to solve this equation! The answer choices present a total of 4 possible numbers to try, and they're all easy to plug back into the problem. We just need to see which ones work! (And be strategic about which ones we try first. For example, we're going to try try –4 first, because if –4 isn't a solution, we'll be able to eliminate three choices.)

$$\frac{2x + 10}{x^2 - x - 6} = \frac{x + 3}{x - 3}$$

$$\frac{2(-4) + 10}{(-4)^2 - (-4) - 6} = \frac{-4 + 3}{-4 - 3}$$

$$\frac{-8 + 10}{16 + 4 - 6} = \frac{-1}{-7}$$

$$\frac{2}{14} = \frac{1}{7}$$

So –4 checks out as a solution. Guess we should try 1 next.

$$\frac{2x + 10}{x^2 - x - 6} = \frac{x + 3}{x - 3}$$

$$\frac{2(1) + 10}{1^2 - 1 - 6} = \frac{1 + 3}{1 - 3}$$

$$\frac{12}{-6} = \frac{4}{-2}$$

$$-2 = -2$$

Welp, 1 worked, too. Choice B must be the answer!

If you prefer to do the math, here it is:

$$\frac{2x + 10}{x^2 - x - 6} = \frac{x + 3}{x - 3}$$

$$\frac{2x + 10}{(x - 3)(x + 2)} = \frac{x + 3}{x - 3}$$

$$\frac{2x + 10}{x + 2} = x + 3$$

$$2x + 10 = (x + 3)(x + 2)$$

$$2x + 10 = x^2 + 5x + 6$$

$$0 = x^2 + 3x - 4$$

$$0 = (x + 4)(x - 1)$$

---

101. B
Working with Advanced Systems of Equations

Calculators are allowed on this one —if you ask me, we *gotta* graph!

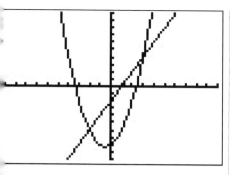

We can almost eyeball the intersections from there, but best to be cautious and let the calculator tell us exactly what they are.

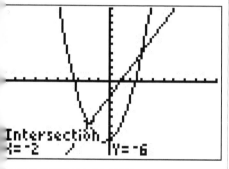

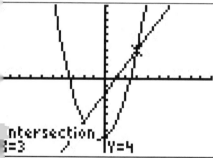

So (x, y) can either be $(-2, -6)$ or $(3, 4)$. That means $|x - y|$ can either be $|-2 - (-6)| = 4$ or it can be $|3 - 4| = 1$.

Obviously the greater of those values is 4, so that's the answer.

102. D
Working with Advanced Systems of Equations

Recognize that the second equation in the system is that of a parabola in vertex form. $y = a(x - h)^2 + k$ is the equation of a parabola with vertex (h, k); the parabola will open upwards if $a > 0$ and downwards if $a < 0$. (Nevermind that the question gives us b and c instead of h and k —test makers *love* to use different letters than we're used to seeing in standard formulas.)

For the system to have no solutions, the graphs of the two equations must not intersect: the parabola must either have a vertex above the horizontal $y = 5$ line and open upwards, or have a vertex below the $y = 5$ line and open downwards. The x-coordinate of the vertex, therefore, doesn't matter at all. We're really only looking at the a and c values here.

In choice A, the vertex is at $(1, 7)$, higher than the $y = 5$ line, and $a < 0$ so it opens down. That will have intersections.

In choice B, the vertex is at $(1, -3)$, lower than the $y = 5$ line, and $a > 0$ so it opens up. That will have intersections.

In choice C, the vertex is at $(-3, 2)$, lower than the $y = 5$ line, and $a > 0$ so it opens up. That will have intersections.

In choice D, the vertex is at $(5, 4)$, lower than the $y = 5$ line, and $a < 0$ so it opens down. That will NOT have intersections, so D is the answer.

103. 64
Functions; Lines

Add a column to the table to have a good look at $g(x)$. Remember, the g values are just 3 times the f values.

x	$f(x)$	$g(x)$
0	24	72
6	22	66
15	19	57

Now, what's the slope of the g line?

$$\text{slope} = \frac{66 - 72}{6 - 0} = \frac{-6}{6} = -1$$

Huh. Well, that's convenient! From there, all we really need to do is count down 2 units from 66 as we count over 2 units from 6 to 8. If the slope of g is –1, and $g(6) = 66$, then:

$$g(7) = 65$$
$$g(8) = 64$$

104. 4
Exponents and Exponential Functions

To start, let's break the left side of the equation into pieces to simplify. First, the numerator of the numerator. When we multiply like bases, we add the exponents.

$$x^a x^2 = x^{a+2}$$

Now let's take care of that whole fraction inside the parentheses on top. When we divide like bases, you subtract the exponents.

$$\frac{x^{a+2}}{x^3} = x^{a+2-3} = x^{a-1}$$

Now we're ready to apply the outer exponent. When we raise a power to a power, we multiply the powers.

$$\left(x^{a-1}\right)^3 = x^{3a-3}$$

Finally, we can incorporate the denominator.

$$\frac{x^{3a-3}}{x^a} = x^{3a-3-a} = x^{2a-3}$$

That's what we can set equal to x^5 to solve for a.

$$x^{2a-3} = x^5$$
$$2a - 3 = 5$$
$$2a = 8$$
$$a = 4$$

Here's that math altogether in case you had a hard time following it piecemeal:

$$\frac{\left(\dfrac{x^a x^2}{x^3}\right)^3}{x^a} = x^5$$

$$\frac{\left(\dfrac{x^{a+2}}{x^3}\right)^3}{x^a} = x^5$$

$$\frac{\left(x^{a-1}\right)^3}{x^a} = x^5$$

$$\frac{x^{3a-3}}{x^a} = x^5$$

$$x^{2a-3} = x^5$$
$$2a - 3 = 5$$
$$2a = 8$$
$$a = 4$$

105. 41
Translating between Words and Math; Measures of Central Tendency and Variability

The first thing we'll want to do here is convert everything to seconds. If the test is 50 minutes long, then it's

$$50 \text{ minutes} \times 60 \, \frac{\text{seconds}}{\text{minutes}} = 3{,}000$$

seconds long. However, Christine's goal is to leave 5 minutes to check her work, and by the same conversion 5 minutes is 300 seconds, so Christine really has 3,000 – 300 = 2,700 seconds to work with.

Remember: we generally know that count of values × average = sum. We can use this to figure out how much time Christine spends on the first 8 and the next 15 questions.

She averages 50 seconds per question on the first 8 questions, so she spends a total of 8 × 50 = 400 seconds on the first 8 questions.

She averages 134 seconds per question on the next 15 questions, so she spends a total of 15 × 134 = 2010 seconds on the next 15 questions.

So far, Christine has done 8 + 15 = 23 questions and spent 400 + 2010 = 2,410 seconds. Therefore, she has 2,700 – 2,410 = 290 seconds left to do the last 7 questions.

She must average $\frac{290}{7} = 41.42...$ seconds per question to finish when she wants to.

Because the question says to round to the nearest second, the answer is 41.

106. 5
Angles, Triangles, and Polygons

Let's make life easier for ourselves and draw the triangle!

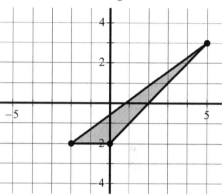

From that, we can see that the base of the triangle, from $(-2, -2)$ to $(0, -2)$ has a length of 2. We can also count up from the base to the point $(5, 3)$ to see that it's a vertical distance of 5 from the base, so the triangle's height is 5.

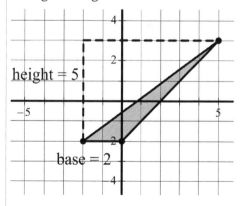

We can use the $A = \frac{1}{2}bh$ formula to calculate the area of the triangle :

172

$$A = \frac{1}{2}(2)(5) = 5$$

and Roman numeral III *must* be true.

Therefore, the answer is choice D.

107. D
Parabolas

There are a few important things to recognize here. First, recognize that the parabola in the graph opens upwards. That tells us that the leading coefficient, a, must be positive. So Roman numeral I must be true.

Since the parabola is in factored form, we know that the zeros of the parabola must therefore be at $x = -b$ and $x = -c$. Because we're told that the absolute value of c is greater than the absolute value of b, we know that the zero that corresponds with c must be the one that's farther away from the origin.

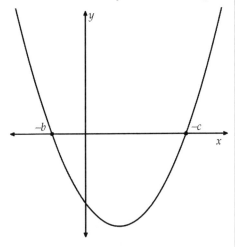

Because $-c$ represents a positive value, c must be negative. Likewise, because $-b$ represents a negative value, b must be positive. If c is negative and b is positive, Roman numeral II *cannot* be true,

108. 40
Solving Systems of Linear Equations

The first step here is to find the intersection point of the two lines that have no unknowns. Since this is a no-calculator question, it's a great opportunity to practice the elimination method of solving systems of linear equations.

$$3x + 4y = 8$$

$$2x + 8y = 4$$

Divide the second equation by 2 to get $4y$ in both equations. This will allow us to subtract and eliminate.

$$3x + 4y = 8$$

$$x + 4y = 2$$

Subtracting tells us that $x = 3$:

$$3x + 4y = 8$$
$$\underline{-(x - 4y) = -2}$$
$$2x + 0y = 6$$
$$x = 3$$

Easy enough to solve for y now:

$$3x + 4y = 8$$

$$3(3) + 4y = 8$$

$$9 + 4y = 8$$

$$4y = -1$$

$$y = -\frac{1}{4}$$

Our last step is just to plug the point $\left(3, -\dfrac{1}{4}\right)$ into the third equation to solve for a:

$10x - ay = a$

$10(3) - a\left(-\dfrac{1}{4}\right) = a$

$30 + \dfrac{1}{4}a = a$

$30 = a - \dfrac{1}{4}a$

$30 = \dfrac{3}{4}a$

$40 = a$

109. C
Absolute Value

The distance between a and b can be expressed using absolute value brackets: $|a - b|$. The twist in this question is that it's about distances from -5, so we want to find an absolute value inequality that either contains $|-5 - x|$ or $|x - (-5)|$, the latter of which of course simplifies to $|x + 5|$. Only choice C contains this, so we're kinda done.

Still, let's just confirm choice C by converting it from an absolute value inequality to a regular inequality range.

$|x + 5| \le 4$

$-4 \le x + 5 \le 4$

Now just subtract 5 from all three parts:

$-9 \le x \le -1$

Indeed, that defines all points a distance of 4 or less from -5.

110. 1
Solving Systems of Linear Equations

Because we're only asked to solve for y, let's see if we can eliminate x. In this case, we can do it in three steps: rearrange the second equation, double it, and then add it to the first equation. Steps 1 and 2:

$5y = 4x - 12$

$-4x + 5y = -12$

$-8x + 10y = -24$

Step 3:

$8x + 3y = 37$

$-8x + 10y = -24$

$0x + 13y = 13$

Of course, from there, we're home free: $y = 1$, and we're done!

111. 6500
Right Triangles and Basic Trigonometry; Binomial Squares and Difference of Two Squares

Remember the complementary angle rule, which tells us that if $\sin x° = \cos y°$, then $x + y = 90$. With that, we're most of the way home.

From there, we'd be fully in the right just to think for a minute about which numbers add up to 90 and multiply to 800. 80 and 10 do, so x and y must be 80 and 10 (or vice versa). What's the value of $80^2 + 10^2$? Easy, that's $6400 + 100 = 6500$.

Another approach is a bit more algebraic; it involves binomial squares. It still requires the initial insight that $x + y = 90$:

$$(x+y)^2 = 90^2$$

$$x^2 + 2xy + y^2 = 8100$$

$$x^2 + 2(800) + y^2 = 8100$$

$$x^2 + 1600 + y^2 = 8100$$

$$x^2 + y^2 = 6500$$

---

112. 165
Measures of Central Tendency and Variability

Average questions like this are usually about sums (number of things times the average equals the sum), so let's figure out how many seconds of music, in total, the musician recorded. If he has 15 songs with an average length of 215 seconds, then in total he has $15 \times 215 = 3{,}225$ seconds of music.

Now we can figure out how many seconds of music the final version of the album will have, based on the given number of minutes and seconds. 48 minutes is $48 \times 60 = 2{,}880$ seconds. Add the last 15 seconds on there and you get 2,895 seconds.

The musician originally recorded 15 songs, and only 13 go on the album, so 2 songs were excluded. To figure out how many seconds of music were excluded, subtract! $3{,}225 - 2{,}895 = 330$ seconds, so there are 330 seconds of music excluded from the final version of the album.

Therefore, the average length of the excluded songs is $\dfrac{330}{2} = 165$ seconds.

---

113. 20
Circles, Radians, and a Little More Trigonometry

No escaping the circle equation here—no way to get this question without knowing $(x - h)^2 + (y - k)^2 = r^2$, where (h, k) is the center of the circle and r is the radius.

Plug the given center and radius into the equation, then manipulate until you get to the form provided in the question. Like so:

$$(x - 5)^2 + (y + 2)^2 = 7^2$$

$$(x^2 - 10x + 25) + (y^2 + 4y + 4) = 49$$

$$x^2 + y^2 - 10x + 4y + 29 = 49$$

$$x^2 + y^2 - 10x + 4y = 20$$

And there we go: 20 is the answer!

---

114. 87
Binomial Squares and Difference of Two Squares

Note that we're given components of a binomial square:

$$(a - b)^2 = a^2 - 2ab + b^2$$

Let's use that to arrive at the answer quickly.

$$a - b = 7$$

$$(a - b)^2 = 7^2$$

$$a^2 - 2ab + b^2 = 49$$

175

Now substitute! We know that $ab = 19$, so we can solve for $a^2 + b^2$:

$$a^2 - 2(19) + b^2 = 49$$

$$a^2 + b^2 - 38 = 49$$

$$a^2 + b^2 = 87$$

---

115. D
Data Analysis 1; Lines

We have to compare the speed at which the hose fills up the tank (6 feet in 4 minutes, so $\frac{6}{4} = 1.5$ feet per minute) and the speed at which the drain empties the tank (6 feet in 3 minutes, so $\frac{6}{3} = 2$ feet per minute). Note: these are the slopes of the two relevant sections of the graph.

Because the drain works faster than the hose, if the hose is turned on and the drain is open at the same time, the tank will end up slowly losing water at a rate of $2 - 1.5 = 0.5$ feet per minute.

If the water is four feet high when the timer starts, and it drains at a rate of 0.5 feet per minute, then the tank will be empty in

$$\frac{4 \text{ feet}}{.5 \text{ feet per minute}} = 8 \text{ minutes.}$$

---

116. D
Ratios and Proportionality

Obviously, we're going to have to convert square meters to square feet (or vice versa) to solve this. But we must be careful! We're given that 1 foot is 0.3048 meters, but that doesn't mean that 1 square foot is

0.3048 square meters! To get that conversion, we must square both values!

$$1 \text{ ft} = 0.3048 \text{ m}$$

$$(1 \text{ ft})^2 = (0.3048 \text{ m})^2$$

$$1 \text{ ft}^2 = 0.09290304 \text{ m}^2$$

NOW we're ready to convert. The apartment on Maple Street that's 715 square feet? Well...

$$715 \text{ ft}^2 \times 0.09290304 \frac{\text{m}^2}{\text{ft}^2} \approx 66.43 \text{ m}^2$$

So the apartment on Maple Street is way smaller than the Apartment on Elm Street:

$$\frac{66.43}{200} \approx \frac{1}{3}$$

Therefore, the answer is D.

---

117. 24
Complex Numbers

Remember that the only way we can multiply two complex numbers and get a real number result is by multiplying complex conjugates. Since we know one of the complex numbers is $5 - 7i$, let's see what happens when we multiply by its complex conjugate, $5 + 7i$.

$$(5 - 7i)(5 + 7i)$$

$$= 25 + 35i - 35i - 49i^2$$

$$= 25 - 49i^2$$

$$= 25 - 49(-1)$$

$$= 74$$

Huh...that's not 148. However, it is *half* of 148! So if we had, for

176

example, $(5-7i)(5+7i)(2)$, that would indeed equal 148.

All we need to do, then, is express $(5-7i)(5+7i)(2)$ in $(5-7i)(a+bi)$ form. All we need to do is distribute the 2!

$(5-7i)(5+7i)(2) = (5-7i)(10+14i)$

That tells us that $a = 10$ and $b = 14$, so $a + b = 24$.

118. A
Lines

A graph is helpful here, but this question was written to be solvable without a calculator—simple line drawings based only on slope and intercept should be enough to arrive at the right conclusions.

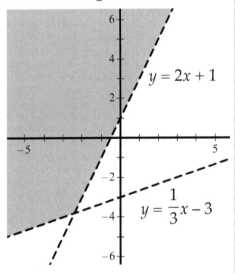

$y = 2x + 1$

$y = \frac{1}{3}x - 3$

From the graph above, we see the solution set, shaded in gray. That's every point that is above *both* lines. Each quadrant has some shaded area except quadrant IV, where $x > 0$ and $y < 0$. Therefore, we can conclude that, if the x-value of the

solution is positive, the y-value must also be positive. In other words, if $a > 0$, then $b > 0$.

119. A
Functions; Lines

When we see function notation in a question involving the xy-plane, we should remember that $f(a) = b$ means that the graph of the f function contains the point (a, b). Practically, what that means for this question is that we know the line in this question contains the points $(3, 8)$ and $(8, 3)$.

What does the line containing those points look like? What's its slope?

$$\text{slope} = \frac{8-3}{3-8} = -1$$

We can derive the equation of the line in slope-intercept form. A line going through $(3, 8)$ with a slope of -1 will have a y-intercept of 11— just count back 3 steps! Therefore, the equation of the line is $f(x) = -x + 11$. Use this equation to test answer choices.

Choice A:

$f(f(4)) = 4$

$f(-4+11) = 4$

$f(7) = 4$

$-7 + 11 = 4$

$4 = 4$

Welp, I guess we're done—choice A worked!

I started with A because that's what I usually do unless the choices are in numerical order, but it's worth noting that a couple choices can probably be eliminated without doing the math based on the fact that you have a line with a negative slope and a positive y-intercept.

For example, C can be knocked right out. Based on the two points you're given, you should be able to see easily that $(-3, -8)$ is nowhere near the line.

B should also be a pretty quick elimination. The only time $f(0) = f(11)$ will be true about a linear function is when the line is horizontal.

So if A didn't work, I'd probably jump right to trying D. But A *did* work—yay!

120. 5
Working with Advanced Systems of Equations

The easiest way to see what's going on in this one is to graph the parabola and the line with a calculator. Here's what they look like on mine after a little window adjustment:

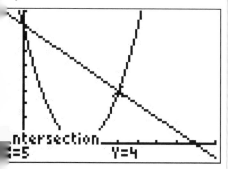

The inequalities tell you that the solution set will be all points below or on the parabola *and* above or on

the line. In other words, the overlapping shaded area below:

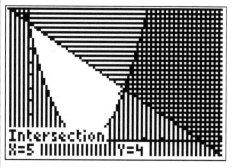

Because a and b are greater than zero, the least possible x-value in that solution set will be the x-value where the parabola and line intersect there in quadrant I. The calculator shows us that the intersection is at $(5, 4)$. Therefore, the answer we seek is 5.

121. 121
Binomial Squares and Difference of Two Squares; Polynomials

Let's start by FOILing:

$4(x - 5)(x + 6) + m$

$= 4(x^2 + x - 30) + m$

$= 4x^2 + 4x - 120 + m$

If that can be rewritten as a binomial square, then we can use the first two terms, $4x^2 + 4x$, to determine what that square must be.

If the first term of the FOILed out square is $4x^2$, then the factored square must look like the following for some constant b:

$(2x + b)(2x + b)$

From there, we can set up an equation to solve.

$$4x^2 + 4x - 120 + m = (2x + b)(2x + b)$$

$$4x^2 + 4x - 120 + m = 4x^2 + 4bx + b^2$$

Because we know that corresponding coefficients of equivalent polynomials are equal, we know that $4 = 4b$, which means that $b = 1$.

Corresponding coefficients rules also tell us that $-120 + m = b^2$. If $b = 1$, then $-120 + m = 1$, which means $m = 121$. That's our answer.

The binomial square at work here is $(2x + 1)^2 = 4x^2 + 4x + 1$.

---

122. A
Functions; Polynomials

Recall that $f(x + 3)$ will be $f(x)$ shifted 3 units to the left. Also recall that zeros in polynomial functions indicate factors: if, as is the case here, a polynomial has a zero at $f(3)$, then $x - 3$ is a factor of that polynomial.

So what we're really doing here is figuring out where the zeros of $f(x + 3)$ will be.

Since $f(x)$ has zeros at $x = 1$ and $x = 3$, a graph shifted 3 units to the left will have zeros at $x = -2$ and $x = 0$.

Therefore, we know that $x + 2$ and x are factors of $f(x + 3)$. The latter is an answer choice, so the answer is A.

A slightly different way to think about this is to think about the factors of $f(x)$ that we know. The table tells us that $x - 1$ and $x - 3$ are factors. In other words, we can partially represent $f(x)$ as follows, using "stuff" as a placeholder for whatever other factors we don't know about:

$$f(x) = (x - 1)(x - 3)(\text{stuff})$$

Similarly, we can partially represent $f(x + 3)$ thusly:

$$f(x + 3) = (x + 3 - 1)(x + 3 - 3)(\text{stuff})$$

$$f(x + 3) = (x + 2)(x)(\text{stuff})$$

There we have it another way: $x + 2$ and x are factors of $f(x + 3)$.

---

123. D
Measures of Central Tendency and Variability

Get this one by elimination—if we can come up with a single example that supports one of these statements, that's good enough to say that it *can* be true.

I.   **The median of the set is a member of the set**—While it's possible for the median of an even-numbered set not to be in the set, the median *can* be in the set when the middle two numbers are equal. For example, the median of {1, 2, 3, 4, 5, 5, 6, 7, 8, 9} is 5.

II. **The sum of the 10 numbers is equal to the average (arithmetic mean) of the 10 numbers**—This *can* be true: it is possible when the sum of the numbers is zero. The average and the sum of {−5, −4, −3, −2, −1, 1, 2, 3, 4, 5} is zero.

III. **The set has 6 modes**—This one *cannot* be true. While a set can have multiple modes, to have 6 modes, we'd need 6 different elements of the set to appear more frequently than the rest of the set. Even if those 6 elements only appeared twice, you're already up to 12 elements without even counting the elements that appear less frequently than twice.

Note that once we come up with examples for I and II, we've logically eliminated every answer choice besides D, so we don't actually need to think about III at all.

---

24. D
Complex Numbers

The only way to get a real number like 130) by multiplying complex numbers is if the complex numbers being multiplied contain conjugates—if they contain something in the form of $a + bi)(a - bi)$.

Of course, because I'm mean, that's not the only thing going on here; it's just our starting point. What if we assume that $a + bi$ is the conjugate of $4 + 7i$, so $a = 4$ and $b = -7$?

$(4 + 7i)(4 - 7i)$

$16 - 28i + 28i - 49i^2$

$16 - 49i^2$

$16 - 49(-1)$

65

Of course, that's not 130. It is, however, *half* of 130, so we're still in business. What that tells us is that we're really dealing with conjugates and a real number multiplied in, too. Like so:

$(4 + 7i)(4 - 7i)(2)$

$= (65)(2)$

$= 130$

The original equation we have doesn't contain a real number multiplied in separately, though, so we need to incorporate it into $a + bi$. Like so:

$(4 + 7i)(a + bi) = (4 + 7i)(4 - 7i)(2)$

$a + bi = (4 - 7i)(2)$

$a + bi = 8 - 14i$

Therefore, $a = 8$, $b = -14$, and $a + b = 8 + (-14) = -6$. There's the answer!

Since we've come this far, let's just confirm that the multiplication works:

$(4 + 7i)(8 - 14i)$

$= 32 - 56i + 56i - 98i^2$

$= 32 - 98i^2$

$= 32 - 98(-1)$

$= 130$

---

125. 972
Working in Three Dimensions

Yikes, right? But really, this isn't so bad, provided we remember a few useful shortcuts for the occasional 3-D problem we might encounter.

First, when a cube is inscribed in a sphere, its long diagonal is the same as the sphere's diameter.

Second, the long diagonal of a cube has a length of $\sqrt{3}$ times the length of one of the cube's edges. (This one is really just a special case of the Pythagorean theorem. It's worth memorizing, just like it's worth knowing that the diagonal of a square is $\sqrt{2}$ times the square's side.)

$V = 972\pi$

Therefore, the value of a is 972.

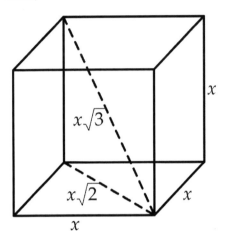

With those useful facts in mind, all we have to do here is calculate the long diagonal/diameter length, divide it by 2 to get the radius, and plug that radius into the formula for the volume of a sphere.

$d = \left(6\sqrt{3}\right)\sqrt{3}$

$d = 18$

$r = 9$

$V = \frac{4}{3}\pi\left(9^3\right)$

$V = \frac{4}{3}\left(729\pi\right)$

Answers

1.	D	51.	A	101.	B
2.	D	52.	6	102.	D
3.	D	53.	C	103.	64
4.	B	54.	6	104.	4
5.	C	55.	3	105.	41
6.	C	56.	5	106.	5
7.	B	57.	D	107.	D
8.	0.8, 4/5	58.	C	108.	40
9.	D	59.	B	109.	C
10.	B	60.	12	110.	1
11.	5	61.	D	111.	6500
12.	B	62.	44	112.	165
13.	A	63.	22	113.	20
14.	A	64.	C	114.	87
15.	A	65.	9	115.	D
16.	B	66.	9.75, 39/4	116.	D
17.	C	67.	.285, .286, 2/7	117.	24
18.	0.75, 3/4	68.	9	118.	A
19.	3	69.	35	119.	A
20.	B	70.	A	120.	5
21.	D	71.	C	121.	121
22.	B	72.	C	122.	A
23.	B	73.	4	123.	D
24.	A	74.	C	124.	D
25.	100	75.	16	125.	972
26.	B	76.	C		
27.	6	77.	D		
28.	A	78.	13		
29.	D	79.	80		
30.	9	80.	D		
31.	C	81.	9		
32.	A	82.	B		
33.	A	83.	B		
34.	B	84.	B		
35.	B	85.	2		
36.	D	86.	55		
37.	C	87.	3.5, 7/2		
38.	A	88.	C		
39.	D	89.	B		
40.	C	90.	B		
41.	88	91.	12		
42.	2	92.	144		
43.	5	93.	144		
44.	3, 10	94.	A		
45.	B	95.	1080		
46.	D	96.	78		
47.	B	97.	12		
48.	0.5, 1/2	98.	B		
49.	C	99.	D		
50.	17	100.	B		